Appliqué & Embroidery FUNDAMENTALS

by Janice Vaine

Landauer Publishing, LLC

by Janice Vaine

Dedication

Thank you, Lord, for Your Grace,
Longsuffering and Lovingkindness.

Psalm 117:2

This book was produced and published by
Landauer Publishing, LLC
3100 101st Street, Urbandale, IA 50322
800-557-2144; www.landauercorp.com

President/Publisher: Jeramy Lanigan Landauer
Vice President of Sales & Administration: Kitty Jacobson
Editor: Jeri Simon
Art Director: Laurel Albright
Designer & Technical Illustrator,
Appliqué & Embroidery Fundamentals: Lisa Christensen
Photography: Sue Voegtlin

Library of Congress Control Number: 2011943408
ISBN 13: 978-1-935726-18-0
ISBN 10: 1-935726-18-8

This book is printed on acid-free paper.
Printed in China by C&C Offset Printing Co., Ltd.
10 9 8 7 6 5 4 3 2 1

Table of Contents

Introduction

Welcome

Appliqué and embroidery, individually and together, have inspired needle artists for centuries. Simple folk art quilts, samplers, and exquisite Baltimore Album quilts have intrigued and inspired with the delicately layered appliqué, clever use of fabrics and color, and at times intricate needlework techniques. After walking the aisles of an exhibit of these extraordinary quilts, we secretly long to achieve what our stitching sisters have accomplished.

Appliqué & Embroidery Fundamentals will teach you the basics of hand appliqué and embroidery techniques. It is for the first-time stitcher, as well as the experienced stitcher who would like to hone their skills. It offers a teaching and learning environment and an opportunity for you to achieve your creative dream.

You will begin In the classroom *with Jan*™ to learn the fundamentals of the time-honored arts of appliqué and embroidery. The classroom lessons will lead you step by step in making the "A" is for Appliqué Pillow, guiding you with clear illustrations and instructions.

After you leave the classroom, you will find the individual alphabet letters artfully encircled by an embellished wreath. Each letter and wreath has a color photograph, tips, a step-by-step chart outlining the stitching order, detailed stitch selection with corresponding stitch instruction page, and suggested fabric, thread, and ribbon supplies.

The next chapter offers eighteen basic embroidery stitches and embellishing techniques to be used in creative ways to embellish each wreath. Each technique has step-by-step instructions and illustrations to walk you through the stitching process.

With each stitch you take, you will gain confidence in your hand appliqué ability and basic embroidery stitches and techniques. Choose among the different techniques to personalize your creative work. The Project section has six projects allowing you the opportunity to showcase your newly acquired skills.

Refer to *The Art of Elegant Hand Embroidery, Embellishment, and Appliqué,* by Janice Vaine for additional appliqué and embellishing techniques and tips.

template
977
110
STAEDTLER
made in U.S.A.
pencil allowance on all openings
Transfer Paper
Papier-Transfert
Papel para Transferencia
Glass Seed Beads
For Needlework Projects
Product of Japan 4 Grams
02104
For Needlework Projects
Product of Japan 4.54 Grams
and NEW Scent-Free!
No Clogging, No Flaking, No Residue
and Completely Acid-Free.
Mary Ellen's
Best Press
The Clear Starch Alternative
Lavender Fields
Shake well, spray on clothing and iron.
KEEP OUT OF REACH OF CHILDREN
Sewline

Supplies

shopping list

The following is a list of the embellishing supplies and tools you will need to accomplish the lessons and projects in the book. Fabric requirements are listed with the individual lessons and projects.

Embroidery Scissors

_____Elan 4" serrated edge embroidery scissors or
_____Karen Kay Buckley's 4" Perfect Scissors®

Embroidery Threads

The Gentle Art 6-stranded cotton floss:
_____#0440 Maple Syrup (wreath)
_____#0110 Dried Thyme (leaves)
_____#0112 Grasshopper (leaves)
_____#0130 Avocado (leaves)
_____#7080 Endive (leaves)
_____#0190 Forest Glade (leaf veins)
_____#7082 Piney Woods (leaf veins)
_____#7023 Green Pasture (flower embellishments)
_____#0320 Old Brick (flower embellishments)
_____#1120 Cherry Bark (flower embellishments)
_____#7008 Rhubarb (flower embellishments)
_____#7014 Antique Rose (flower embellishments)
_____#7019 Pomegranate (flower embellishments)
_____#7020 Butternut Squash (flower embellishments)
_____#7041 Apple Cider (flower embellishments)
DMC Perle Cotton No. 5 or 8
(color to match fabric of Spider Web Roses)

The Gentle Art Simply Wool:
_____#0130-W Avocado (leaves)
_____#0440-W Maple Syrup (wreath)

Loew-Cornell® Graphite and White Transfer Paper

5" and 10" Morgan No-Slip Hoops®

Mary Ellen's Best Press™

Mill Hill® Glass Beads for flower centers:

_____#62041 Frosted Glass Beads
_____#03046 Antique Glass Beads
_____#02002 Glass Seed Beads
_____#00968 Glass Seed Beads
_____#02077 Glass Beads
_____#02076 Glass Seed Beads
_____#02080 Glass Seed Beads

Needles

_____#10 Betweens for needleturn
_____#9 Crewel for embroidery
_____#22 Chenille for silk ribbon embro
_____#11 Milliners or Straw for bullions
_____#10 Sharps for Perfect Placement Appliqué
_____#22 Tapestry for woven embroidery stitches

Patchwork Pins by Clover, extra fine

Staedtler® Mars® Combo Circle Template or Karen Kay Buckley Perfect Circles®

Ribbons

Superior 2mm Silk Ribbon:
_____#SRV-02-129 Serengeti (wreath)

Superior 4mm Silk Ribbon:
_____#SRV-04-107 Daffodil (flower centers)
_____#SRV-04-114 Eucalyptus (leaves)
_____#SRV-04-116 Sage (leaves)
_____#SRV-04-131 Vine (leaves)
_____#SRV-04-120 Bachelor Buttons (flowers)

Superior 7mm Silk Ribbon:
_____#SRV-07-103 Hyacinth (flowers)
_____#SRV-07-127 A Dozen Roses (flowers)

French Ribbon Variation:
_____#0035-2 (flowers)
_____#0035-7 (flowers)
_____#0035-10 (flowers)
_____#0035-12 (flowers)

French Ombré Wired Ribbon:
_____#48-3 (flowers)
_____#11194-140 (flowers)
_____#00471-63 (flowers)
_____#1100-828 (flowers)
_____#49-1 (flowers/leaves)
_____#49-12 (leaves)
_____#49-7 (leaves)
_____#48-9 (leaves)

Sandpaper Board

Sewline™ Fabric Mechanical Pencil Trio
includes stylus, white, & graphite ceramic markers

Skinny Mini Tube Turner by Mary Kay Perry Designs™

Threads

_____YLI Quilting Thread, Natural
_____Superior Threads Kimono Silk
or YLI Silk 100, colors to match appliqué fabric
_____50 wt. cotton thread in colors to match
flower fabrics

In the classroom *with Jan*™

Welcome to my classroom. In this chapter, we will walk together through the basics of hand appliqué and embroidery.

We will begin with Perfect Placement Appliqué. Using the letter A, you will learn the basics of hand appliqué, including threading the needle and knotting the thread, the appliqué stitch, points, corners, curves, and reverse appliqué.

Next you will practice the fundamentals of embroidery as I suggest ways to embellish the wreath that encircles the A. I will guide you through threading and knotting silk ribbon, separating embroidery flosses, correctly placing your block in an embroidery hoop, and the embroidery stitches themselves. You will learn all the techniques and tips you need to successfully complete the block.

Once your block is complete, I will teach you a simple way to display your needlework skills on an exquisite pillow.

The following pages will guide you step by step in the fundamentals of hand appliqué and embroidery. By the end of our time together, you will have the confidence to stitch any block within the pages of this book and be creatively inspired to continue your needlework journey.

Let's get started.

Perfect Placement Appliqué

Preparing the Appliqué

Perfect Placement Appliqué is an efficient method in both time and materials to prepare fabric for hand needleturn appliqué. This method offers accurate results. It makes working on your blocks convenient and portable, affording you less preparation time and more stitching time.

Supplies for "A" Block

Fabric: Fat quarter for background
Fat quarter for wreath stem and leaves
¼ yard for flowers and berries
6" x 6" square of batting

Threads & Ribbons: Quilting thread in a contrasting color to appliqué fabrics
Appliqué threads in colors to match appliqué fabrics; I recommend Kimono Silk by Superior Threads or YLI silk 100 thread (color #235 blends with most fabrics)
6-stranded cotton embroidery floss (leaves)
4mm silk ribbon for leaves

Needles: #10 Betweens for needleturn appliqué
#9 Crewel for embroidery
#22 Chenille for silk ribbon embroidery
#10 Sharps for perfect placement appliqué

Notions: 10" embroidery hoop (I recommend Morgan No-Slip Hoops®)
Loew Cornell® transfer paper
Sewline™ Fabric Mechanical Pencil Trio (includes white and graphite ceramic markers and stylus)
Staedtler® Mars® Combo Circle Template (available at office supply stores)

The Background Fabric

1 Cut a 13" x 13" piece of background fabric using a pinking rotary cutter blade. Using a pinking blade will stop the edges of the fabric from fraying as you work on the block.

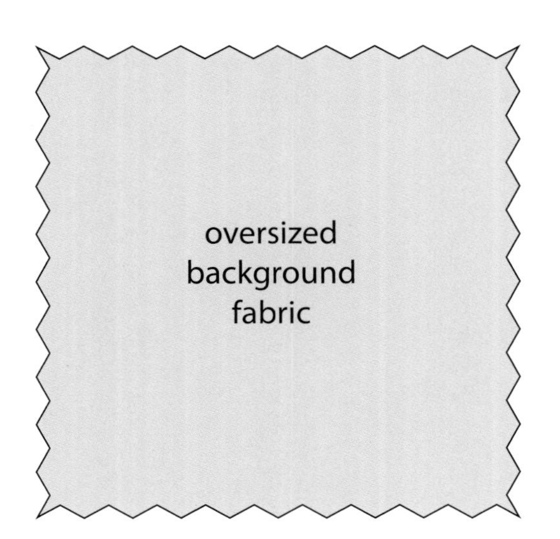

2 Fold the fabric in half vertically and horizontally. LIGHTLY finger press centerlines.

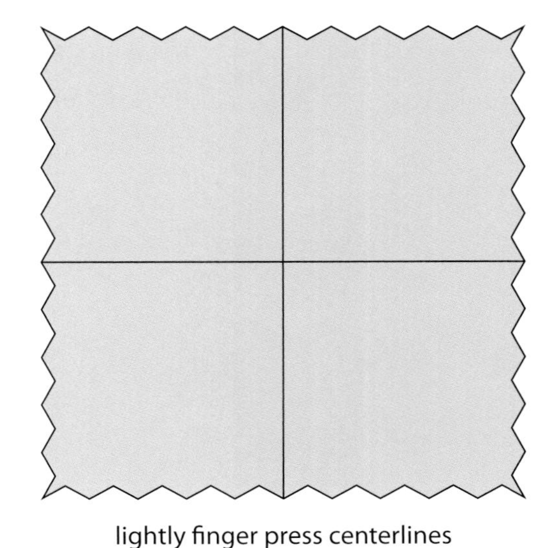

lightly finger press centerlines

Tip *Always oversize your background fabric for appliqué by 1" to allow for stitching shrinkage. If the block will include embroidered embellishment, make sure the background fabric will fit in an embroidery hoop that encompasses the whole design. The designs included in this book are for 9" finished blocks. They were stitched on 13" x 13" background fabric and a 10" embroidery hoop was used for embellishments.*

Transferring Pattern Designs

The "A" block pattern can be found on page 39.

1 Place the background fabric on a flat surface right side up. Center the pattern on top of the background fabric, right side up, matching the pattern's horizontal and vertical lines with the finger pressed lines on the background fabric. Pin in place.

background fabric right side UP
pattern right side UP

2 Place the transfer paper on a flat surface, carbon side up.

transfer paper carbon side UP

3 Place the pinned fabric and pattern on top of the transfer paper. Using a stylus, trace the entire pattern.

4 Check the wrong side of the fabric to be certain the full pattern has been transferred. The pattern is reversed and ready to appliqué. When completely traced, remove pins.

wrong side of background fabric
with transferred design

The Appliqué Fabric

An appliqué design is worked from the bottom to top. In other words, if design elements overlap the bottom pieces are appliquéd first. The sequence for the A wreath will be the letter A, followed by the embellished wreath, including the stem, leaves, berries, and embellished flowers.

1 Cut a 6" x 6" square of fabric for the A. Place it on a flat surface right side down on the diagonal. Place the background fabric, right side down, on top of the A fabric, centering the traced A. Pin in place.

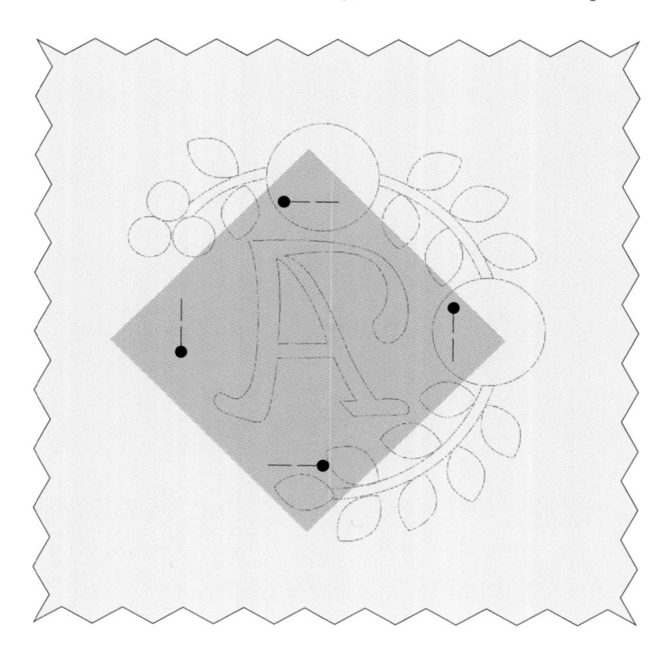

2 Thread a #10 Sharps needle with quilting thread in a color easily seen on the A fabric. Knot the end of the thread. Baste stitch the A fabric and background fabric together along the drawn line. The knot and a short length of thread are on the right side of the A fabric.

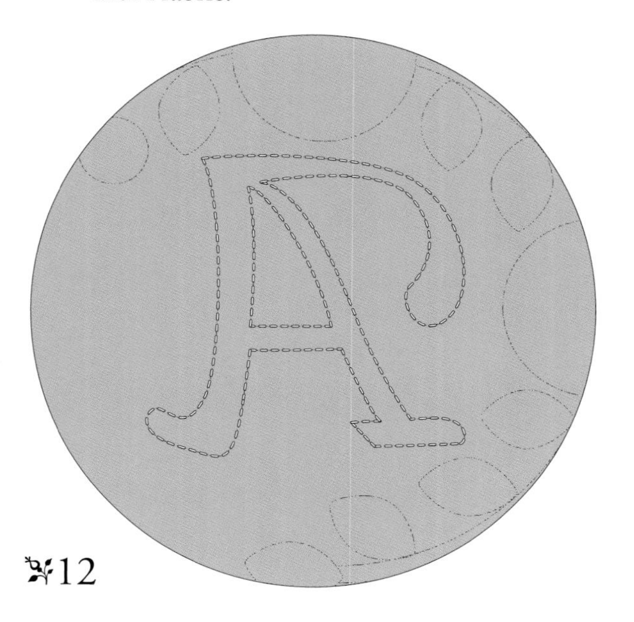

3 On the right side of the A fabric, use a marking pencil to trace along the outside edge of the basting stitches.

Tip *Place the basted background and A fabrics on a sandpaper board when tracing around basting stitches for a smooth traced line.*

4 Trim the appliqué fabric only, leaving a 3⁄16" seam allowance – smaller than a ¼" but larger than an ⅛". DO NOT TRIM the triangle in the center of the A at this time.

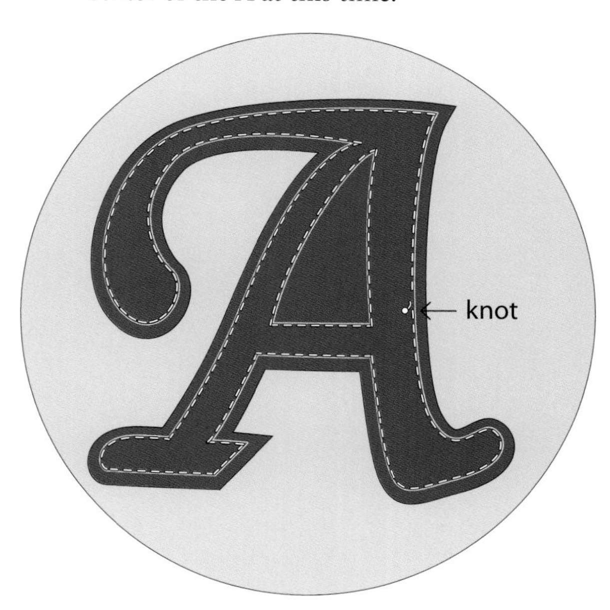

Tip *Draw a 3⁄16" seam allowance on the outer edge of your background fabric. This will help you visualize the amount of fabric to leave when trimming your seam allowance.*

A Word about Basting

Accurately basting your appliqué pieces to the background fabric will give you precise finished results.

The beginning point of your basting will be the beginning point of your appliqué. The knot and thread tail will indicate your beginning point on the right side of the appliqué fabric.

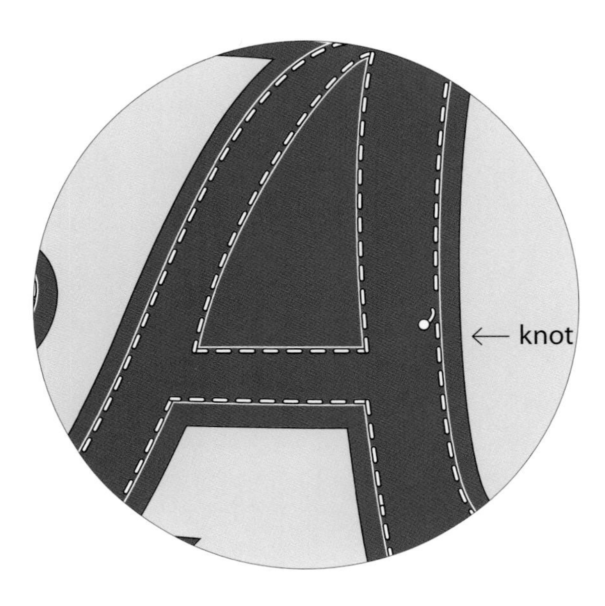

Always begin basting (and appliquéing) on the straightest edge available. Never begin on a curve, at a point, or at an inside corner.

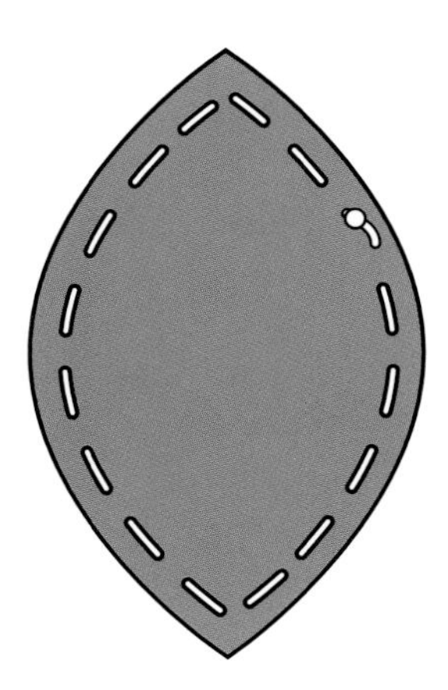

Basting stitches should be small enough to define the appliqué shape, yet large enough to speed application. Remember, the basting stitches will eventually be cut and removed, so we do not want to spend a lot of time making tiny basting stitches.

The basting stitches need to accurately indicate points and corners. Therefore, be sure to take your needle down or bring it up on the exact points and inside corners.

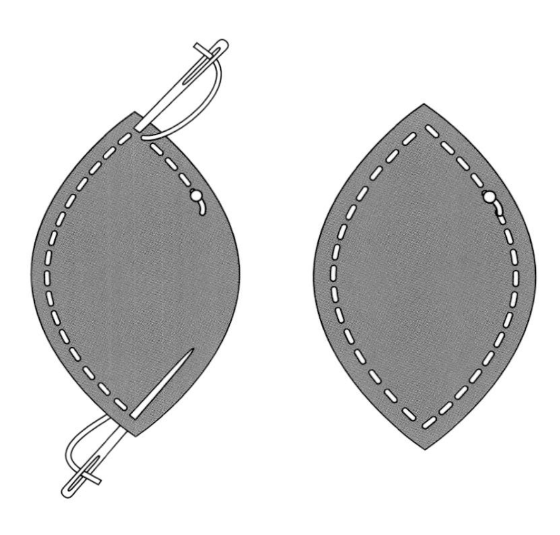

The basting stitches along curves should be slightly smaller to accurately define the smooth lines of the curve.

Appliquéing by Hand

Needle & Thread

Now that the A is ready to appliqué, you need to thread a needle and knot the thread to begin stitching. Use a #10 Betwee needle and 100 weight silk thread. I recommend Superior Kimono silk thread or YLI Silk 100 in a color to match your appliqué fabric. A knot at the eye of the needle will keep the silk thread from sliding out of the eye of the needle as you stit

Knot at the Eye of the Needle

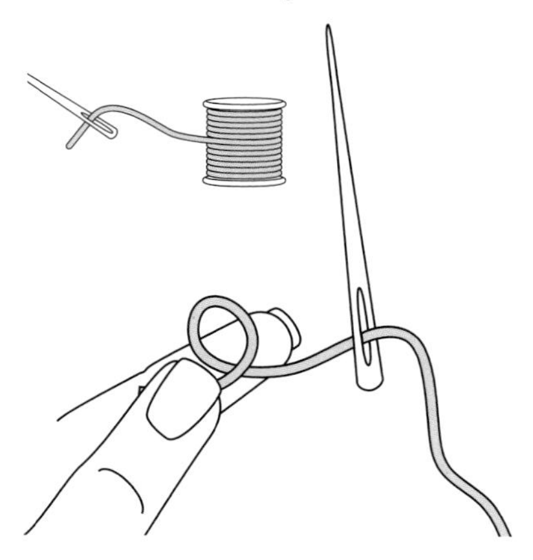

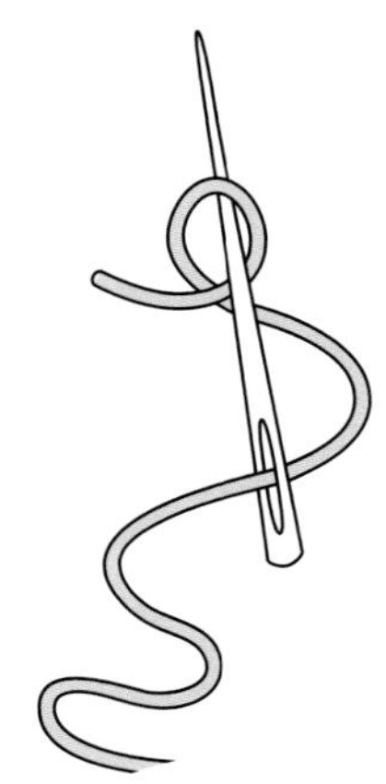

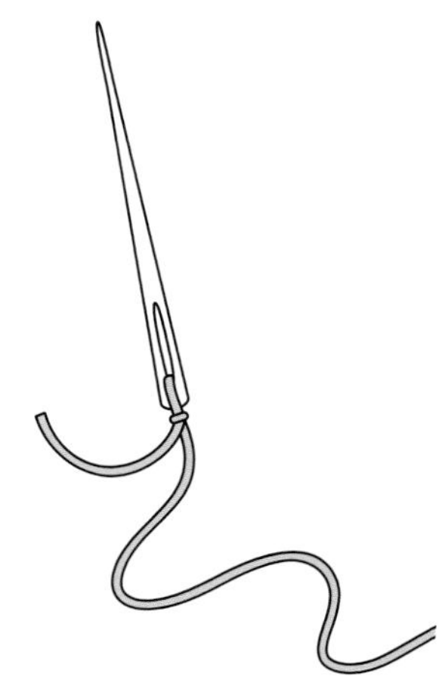

1. Pull the thread off the spool and place it through the eye of the needle. With the short tail end of the thread, make a loop on the pad of your forefinger.
2. Pass the needle through the loop, front to back.
3. Pull the short tail end of the thread to make a tiny knot at the eye of the needle.
4. Cut a length of thread off the spool measuring the distance from the eye of the needle held between the thumb and forefinger to the elbow (approximately 18"). This length will keep the thread from fraying and breaking while stitching.

Knotting the End of the Thread

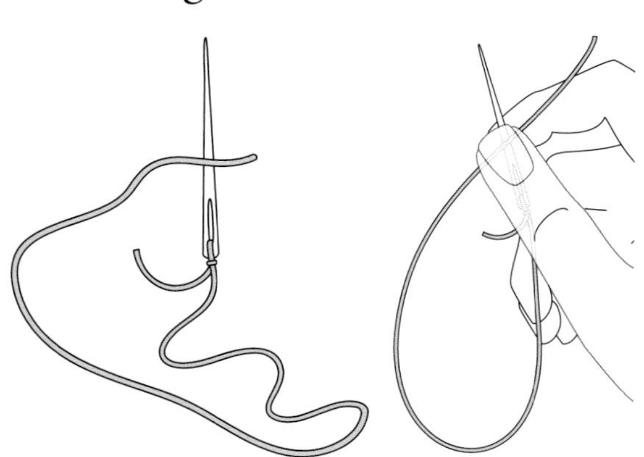

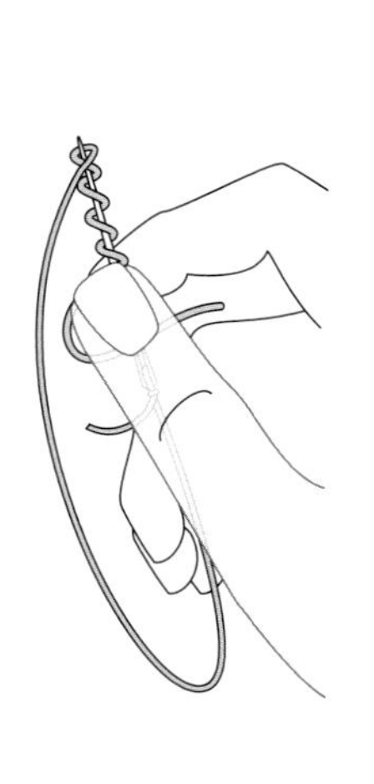

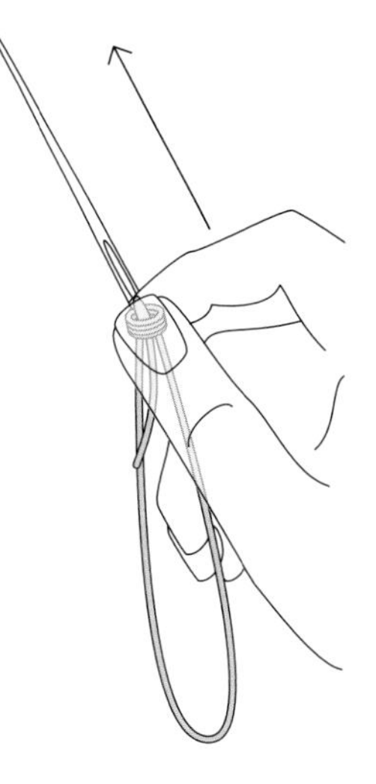

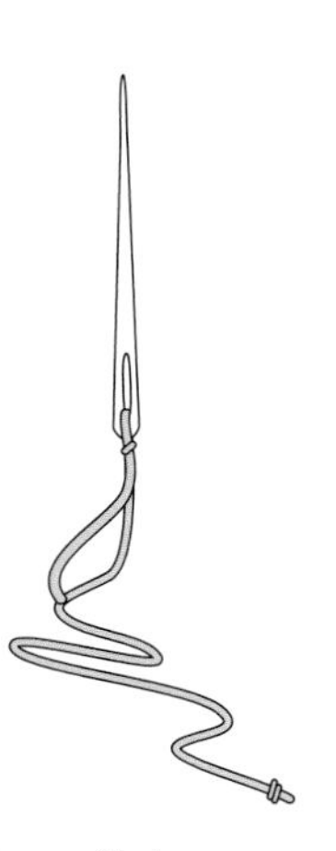

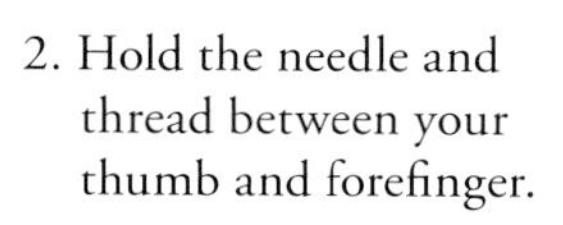

1. Place the end of the thread over the needle making a cross.
2. Hold the needle and thread between your thumb and forefinger.
3. Wrap the working thread clockwise around the needle, ten times for silk thread, five times for cotton thread.
4. Hold the wraps on the needle between your thumb and forefinger, pull the needle up, holding the wraps under your thumb and fingernail…
5. …all the way to the end, making a perfect knot. This is also known as the Quilter's Knot.

The Appliqué Stitch

You are now ready to appliqué. The stitch used in hand appliqué to join the appliqué to the background fabric is the tack stitch. This stitching process is also referred to as needleturn appliqué. With practice, needleturning and stitching will become second nature. The needle will effortlessly turn seam allowances and tiny stitches will disappear unnoticed into the fabric.

1 Place the threaded needle between the appliqué and background fabric at the beginning knot of the basting stitches. Bring the needle and thread to the front of the appliqué fabric on the drawn line at A. This hides the thread knot between the appliqué fabric and the background.

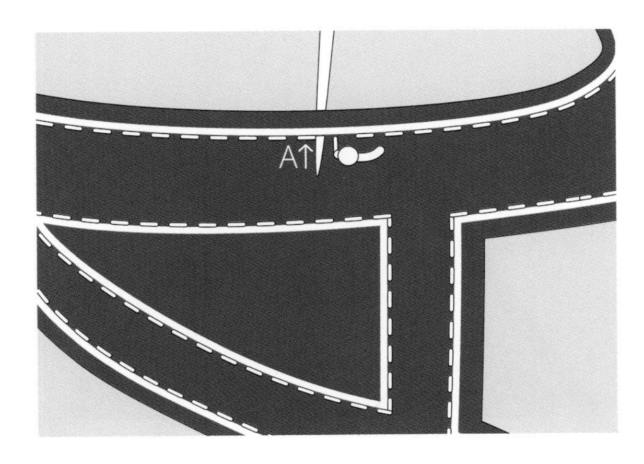

2 Clip the beginning knot of the basting thread. On the wrong side of the background fabric, use the tip of the needle to pull out a ½" length of basting stitches. The number of stitches to remove will depend on the length of the basting stitches. A short distance of the appliqué seam allowance is now ready to be turned under with the tip of your needle.

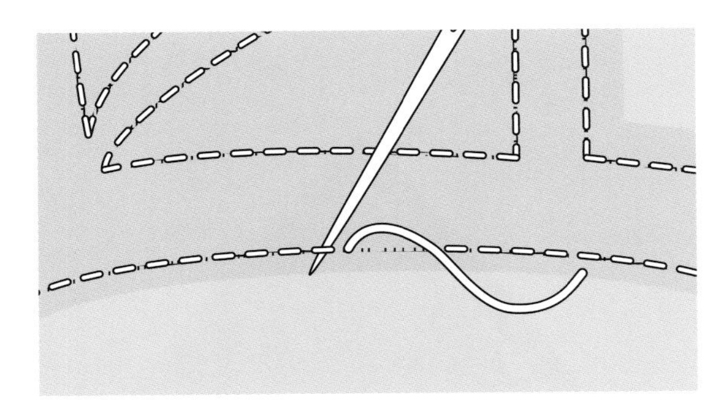

Tip *Pulling the basting thread to the back of the fabric will eliminate the need to continually clip basting threads and creating numerous loose thread snippets.*

3 On the right side of the background fabric, use the needle to sweep under a small ¼" section of the 3⁄16" seam allowance, holding it in place with the thumbnail. Turn under only a ¼" length of seam allowance at a time. Concentrating on this small section of the appliqué makes it less likely to develop unwelcome bumps or tucks, maintaining smooth curves and lines.

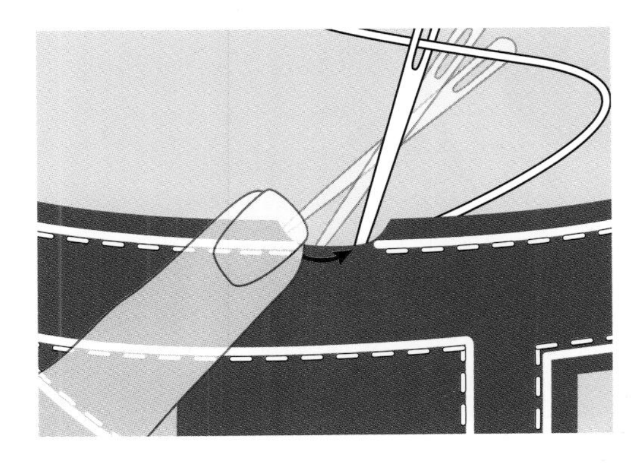

4 Take the tip of the needle to the back at B (into the background fabric only, right next to the applique fabric) and out at C (approximately three thread widths into the appliqué fabric).

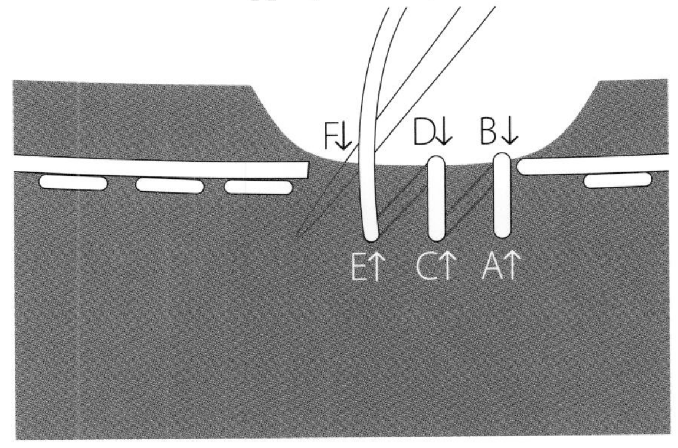

5 Following step 4, continue working along the edge of the appliqué fabric, keeping the appliqué stitches perpendicular to the edge of the appliqué. Use the tip of the needle to remove basting stitches and turn under small amounts of the seam allowance as you progress around the appliqué. When you reach the last 3" of the thread, take the needle and thread to the back and end the stitching following the instructions on page 22.

Outside Corners

Stitching outside corners, or points, is one of the most common appliqué techniques. You will find outside corners in every design, from tips of leaves to the ends of stems. As you work toward the first outside corner on the A the following lesson will guide you and give you the confidence to handle any point.

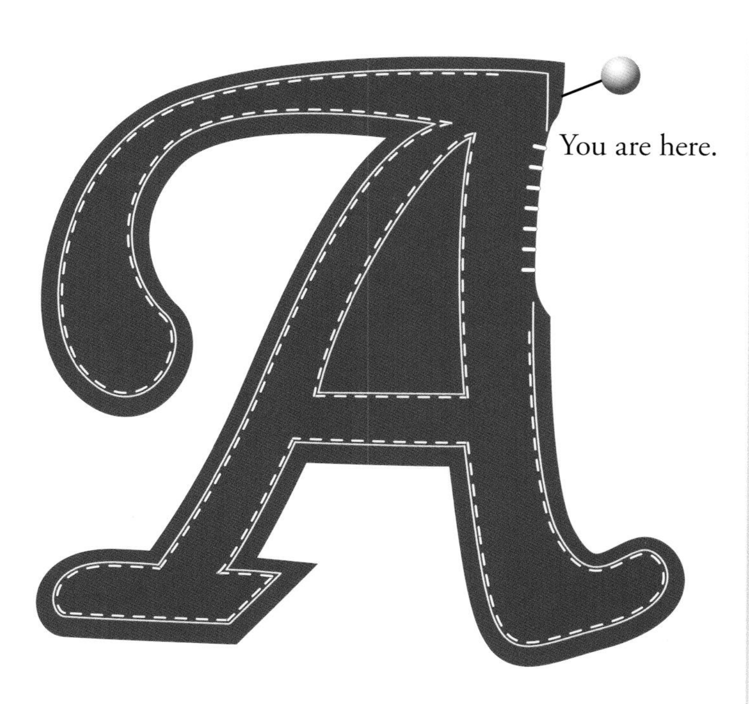

1 As you approach the outside corner, remove the basting stitches through the point and ¼" down the opposite side.

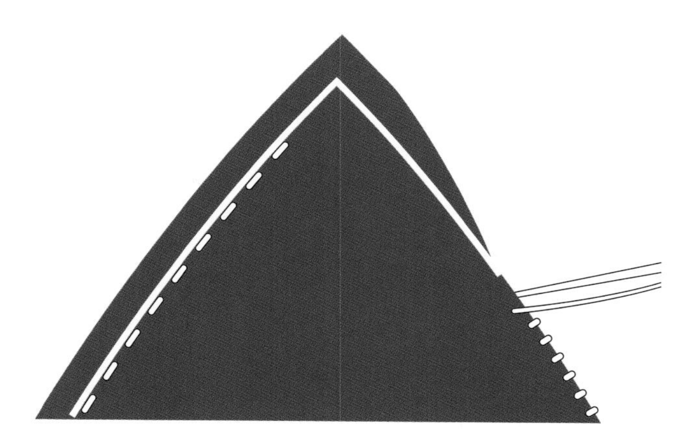

2 Using the tip of the needle, turn the seam allowance under from the corner down to the straight edge to your stitching. Finger press.

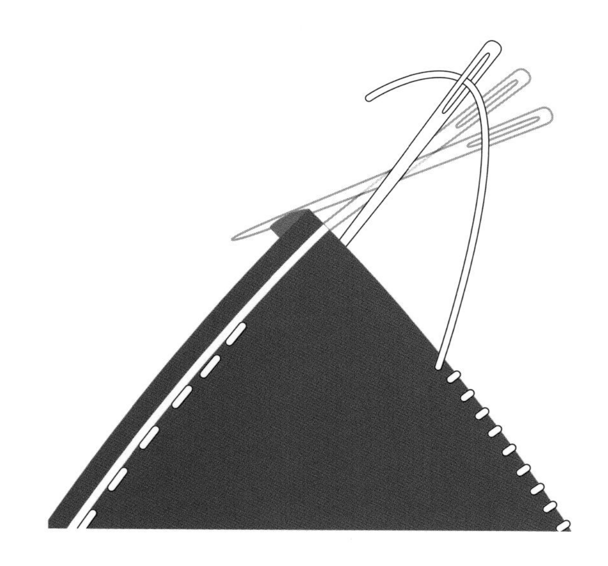

3 Appliqué to the corner, making the stitches closer together the last ¼" up to the point. Take the last stitch directly in the point. If there is a little "dog ear" sticking out at the end of the seam allowance, cut it even with the seam allowance. Do not make the seam allowance smaller.

Outside Corners *continued*

4 Place the point of the needle in the seam allowance of the appliqué fabric only. If the fabric is a tight weave and not fraying, make a small "stitch" in the seam allowance only with the tip of the needle close to the right edge. If the fabric is a loose weave, use the point of a wooden toothpick, skewer or the points of the blades of small, sharp embroidery scissors to turn and sweep the seam allowance under.

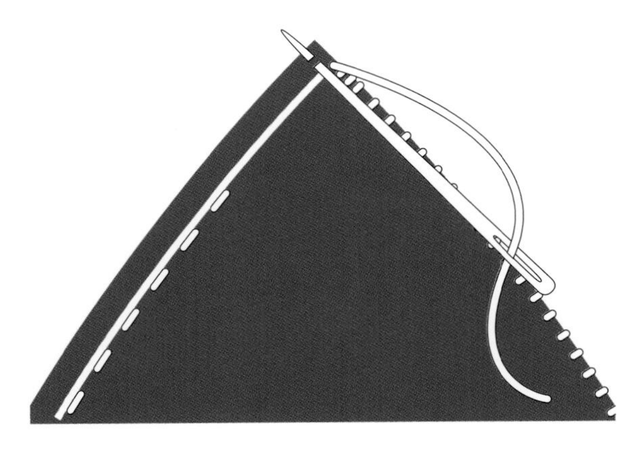

5 Turn the needle 180-degrees down and under the seam allowance, pushing the needle with the appliqué fabric up against the tightly stitched right edge of the appliqué fabric.

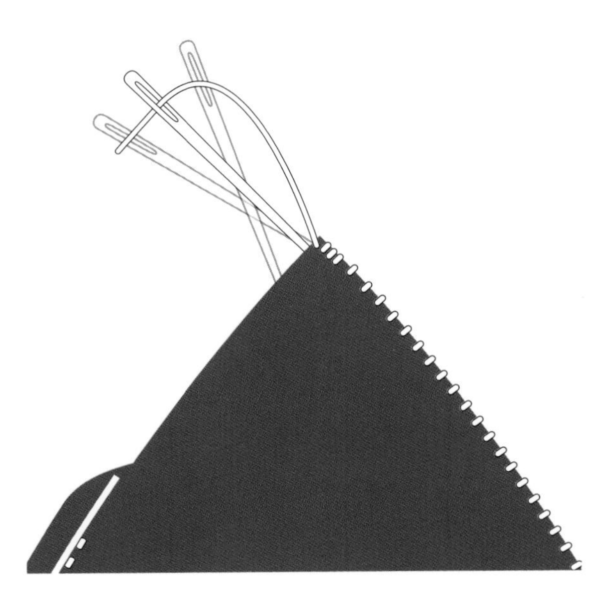

6 Keeping the needle and fabric pressed up against the right edge seam, place your thumb over the corner and finger press.

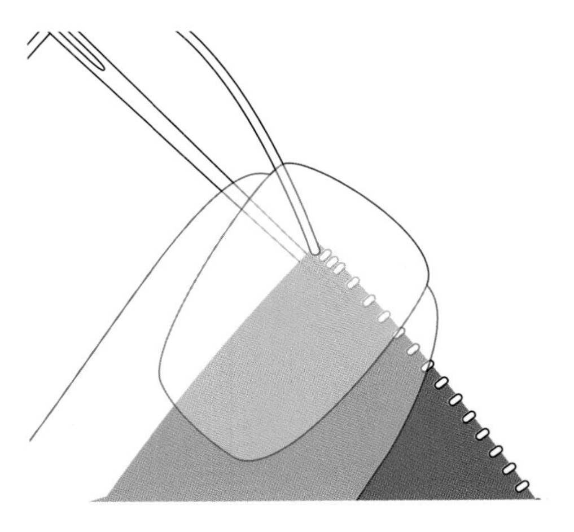

7 Pull the needle and thread upward to "pop" out the corner and create a perfect point.

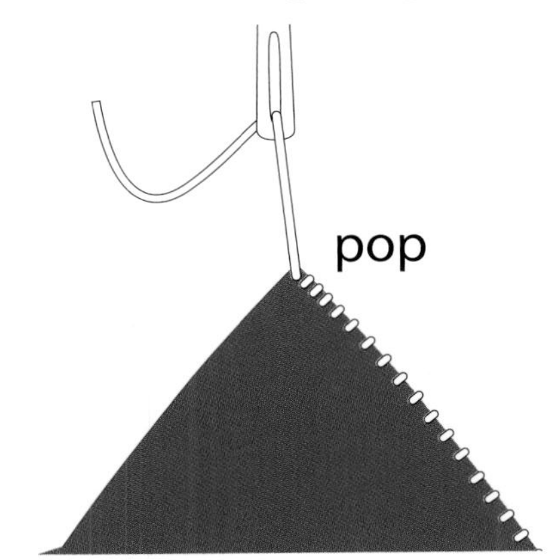

8 Make a slightly elongated stitch in the corner. This tiny elongated stitch gives the allusion of a sharp, crisp corner. Take three small stitches working down the opposite side of the point. Continue needleturning and stitching across the top of the A.

Outside Curves

As you continue working around the outside edge of the A, the next appliqué technique you will learn is Outside Curves. When placing the appliqué fabric on the diagonal and basting it to the background fabric, you were taking advantage of the bias grain of the fabric. When appliqué fabric is cut on the bias, it helps prevent fraying and allows the fabric to easily turn under for smooth curves.

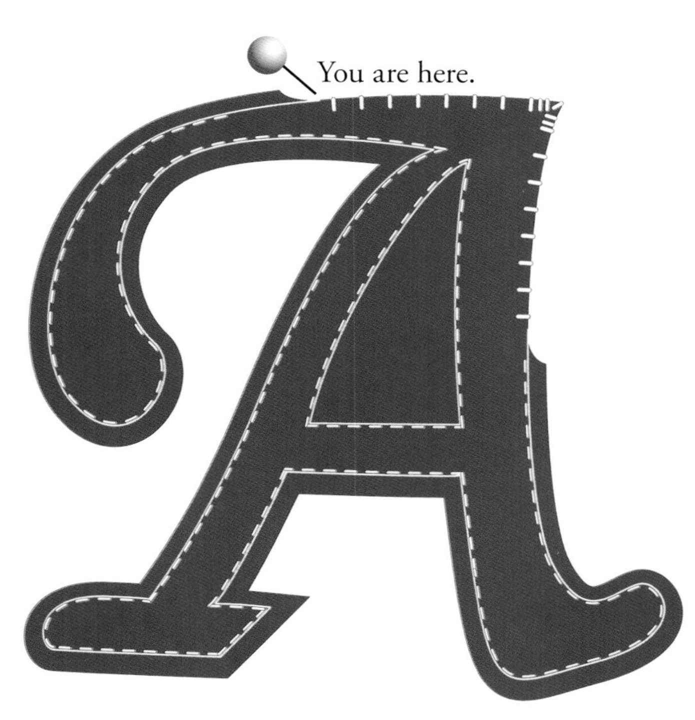

1 When appliquéing outside curves, remove only a small section of basting stitches at a time. You will work no more than ⅛" of the curve at a time. Gently sweep the seam allowance under, holding the small ⅛" distance in place with your thumbnail.

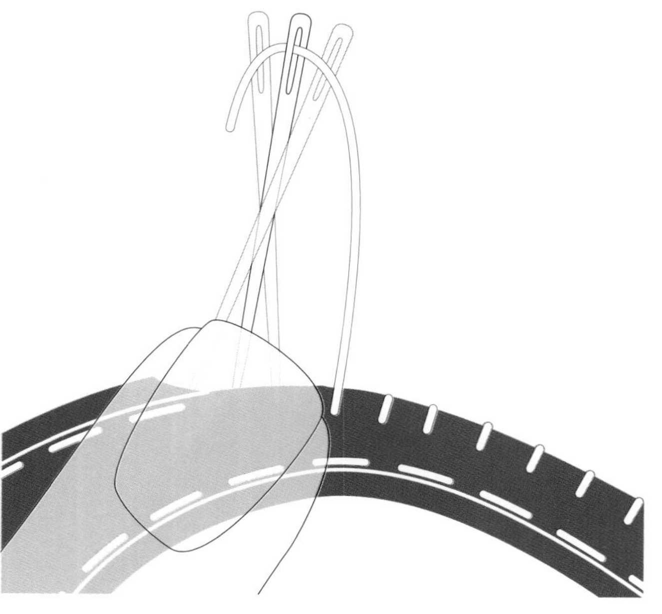

2 As you work around the curve, keep the appliqué stitches closer together than your normal stitch. This helps keep the curve smooth.

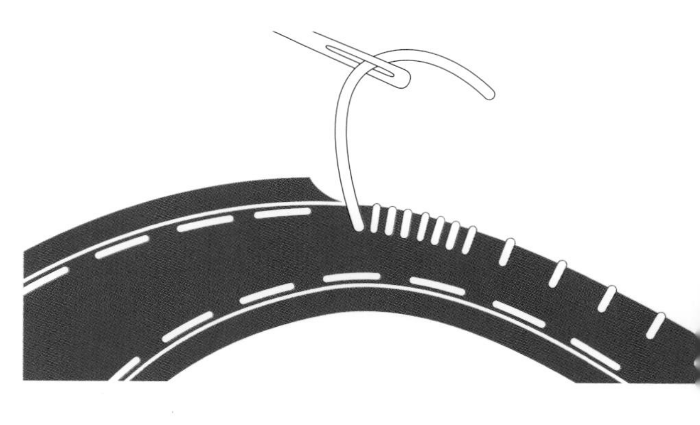

3 Continue stitching down and around the outside curve.

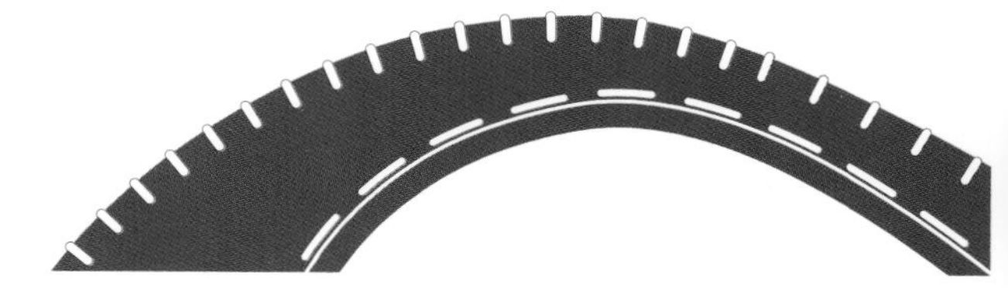

Tip *If a point, bump, or pleat appears when you turn under the seam allowance, use your needle to smooth it out before you stitch. Taking a stitch when there is a point, bump, or pleat will not remove it, but will permanently stitch it in place.*

4 Stitch around the tip of the curve remembering to keep your stitches close together.

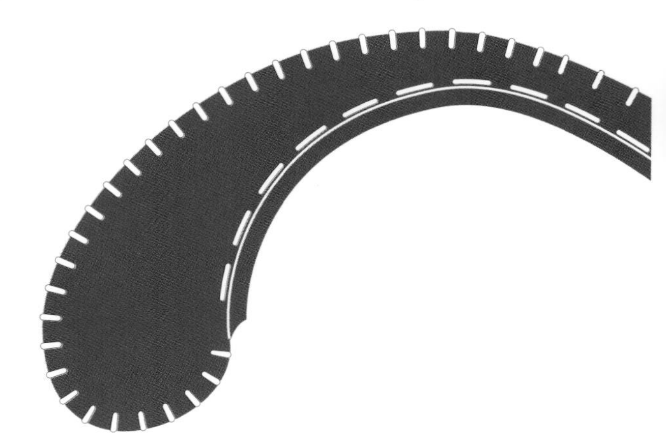

Inside Curves

You have worked down and around the outside curves of the A and are now approaching the first inside curve. The cut bias edge of a gentle inside curve will normally turn under smoothly without clipping. However, if an inside curve is narrow or the seam allowance does not lie smoothly once it has been swept under, it may be necessary to clip the seam allowance.

1 Clip the seam allowance of the inside curve. The clips should be within two to three threads of the drawn line. The fabric between the clips become little tabs in the seam allowance.

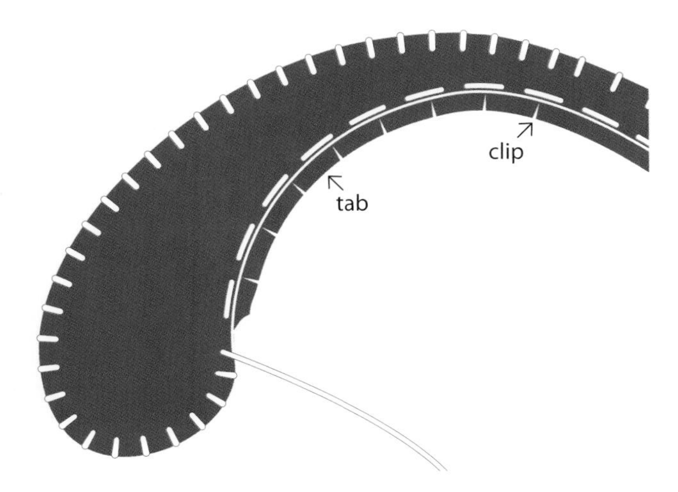

Tip *Do not clip the appliqué fabric until you are ready to stitch the inside curve. This helps prevent the curve from fraying.*

2 When sweeping under the clipped seam allowance of an inside curve, place the needle in the middle of a tab and sweep the seam allowance under. Never turn the seam allowance under by placing the needle in the clip as this will fray the fabric to or beyond the seam allowance.

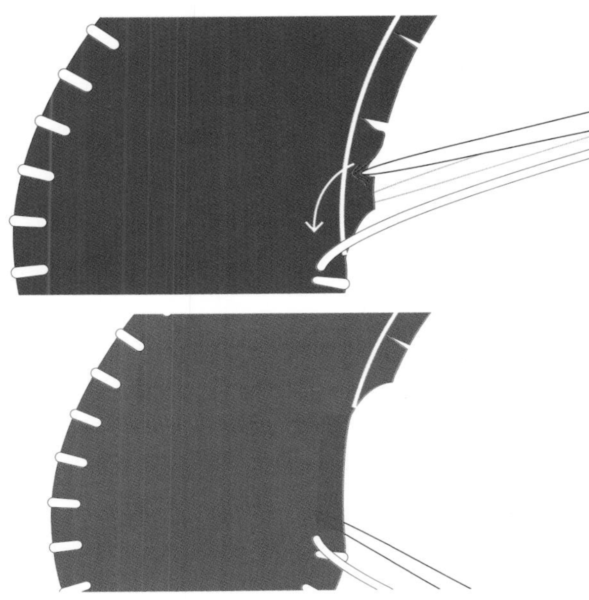

3 Continue needleturning and appliquéing the inside curve as you stitch toward the first inside corner.

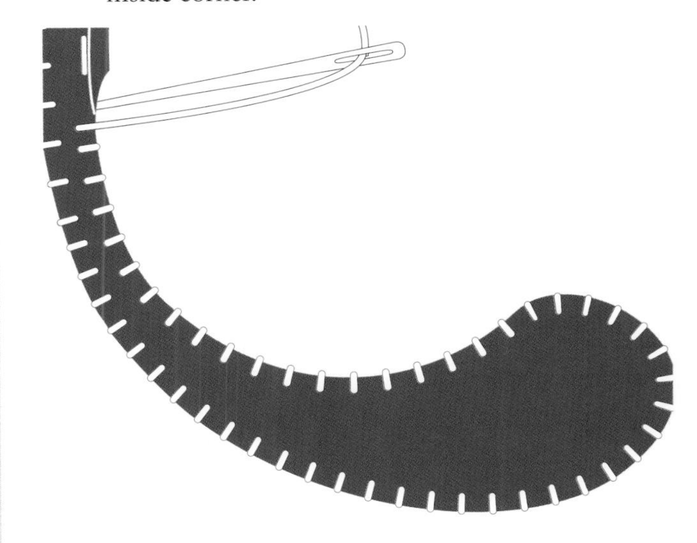

In the classroom *with Jan*™

Inside Corners

You have worked around the outside and inside curves and are approaching the first inside corner. There are eight inside corners on the A, so you will become quite proficient at inside corners. The secret to beautiful appliqué is practice. The more you appliqué, the more skilled you will become at this gentle needlework.

1 As you work toward the inside corner at the top of the A, remove the basting stitches through the inside corner and the beginning of the uphill climb out of the valley. Work appliqué stitches down into the corner until the seam allowance will no longer turn under.

Tip *When approaching an inside corner, do not clip the appliqué fabric until you are ready to stitch the inside corner. This will help prevent the corner from fraying.*

2 When the seam allowance will no longer turn under, clip into the corner to within one fabric thread of the marked corner, or the bottom of the V. Appliquè to the clip, making the last three stitches closer together. The last stitch is taken just to the right of the clip at the inside corner.

3 Take the needle down at A and up at B, approximately three threads inside the clip. This upcoming stitch is an elongated stitch. It is directly in the corner and slightly longer than the standard appliqué tack stitch. Pull the needle and thread through the fabric.

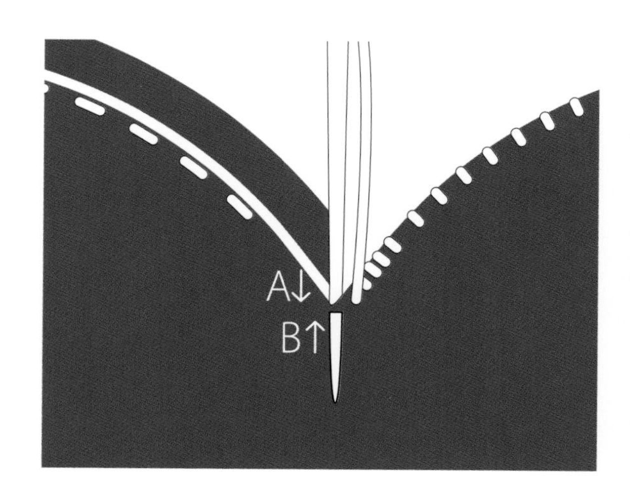

Inside Corners *continued*

4 Take the needle to the back at A and up at B, in the same hole as in the previous step. Pull the needle and thread through the fabric.

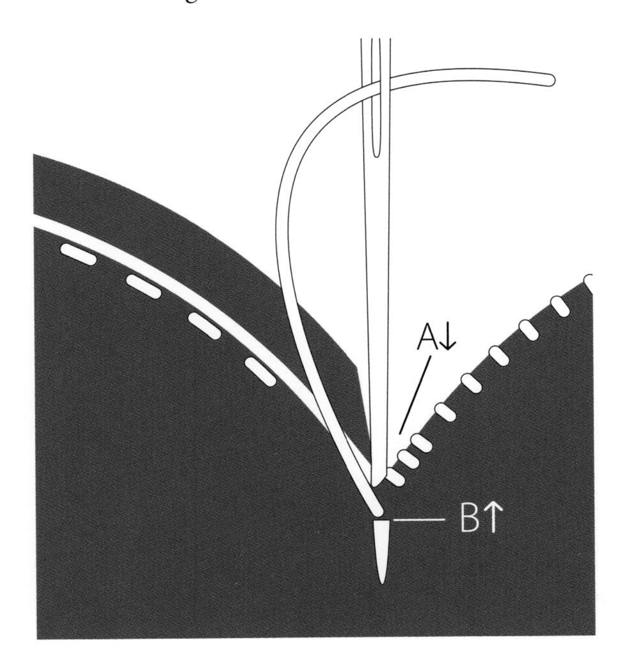

5 Sweep the needle between the background and appliqué fabric. Do not pierce the background fabric with the needle.

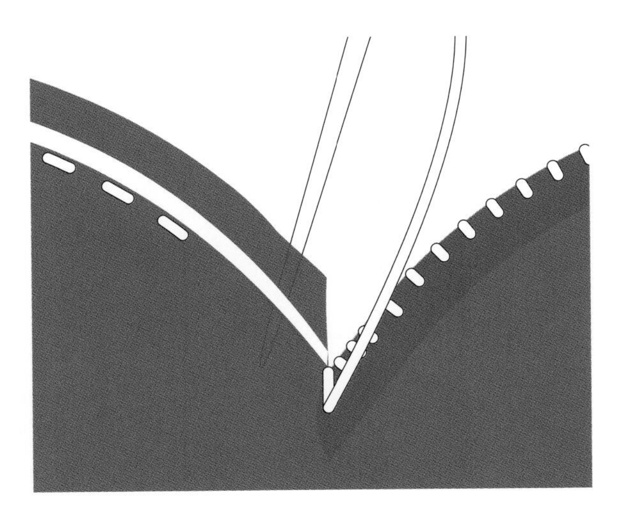

6 Bring the needle and thread up through the appliqué fabric at B (the same hole as in step 4), and gently pull the working thread, rolling the appliqué fabric seam allowance under.

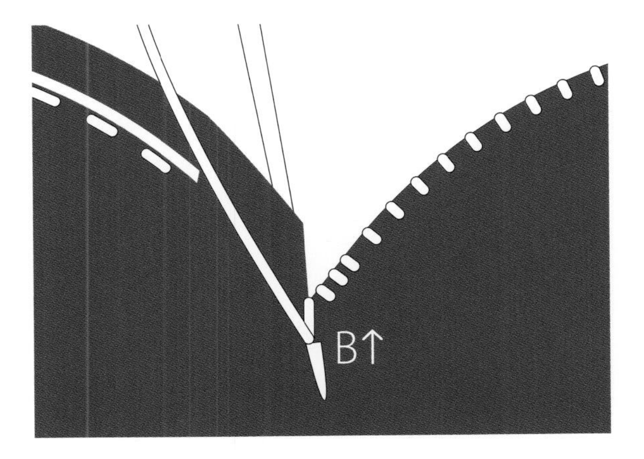

7 Using the tip of the needle, sweep the uphill climb seam allowance under. Continue needleturning and stitching the seam allowance under.

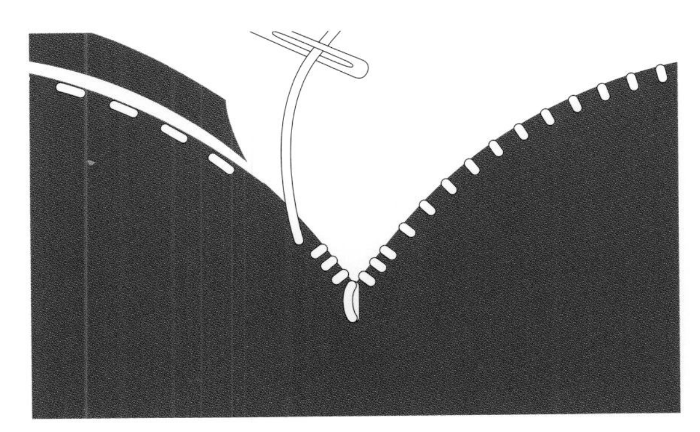

Tip *If you find a little "hair" of fabric at an inside corner, stick your needle into a glue stick. Use the glue covered needle to "sweep" the hair under the seam. Finger press and stitch the corner.*

Tip *A bottle of clear nail polish can help prevent the fabric edges and corners from fraying. Remove excess polish from the brush. LIGHTLY brush the fabric with the clear polish along the seam allowance cutting line (i.e., 3⁄16" from the drawn pattern line). Be careful not to apply polish on the turn line, which would make it difficult to needleturn. Allow to dry. Cut out the appliqué with a 3⁄16" seam allowance. Clip the inside corner only when it is time to stitch.*

Ending the Stitching & Beginning Again

Continue appliquéing your A, practicing the techniques you have learned for corners and curves. As you complete your appliquéd A, remove the last of the basting stitches and turn under the final portion of the seam allowance. Make sure there is a smooth transition to the beginning appliqué stitches. Appliqué to your beginning stitches and end the stitching.

Ending the Stitching

1 Take the needle and thread to the wrong side of the background fabric. Make a small stitch in the background fabric, being careful not to catch the appliqué fabric on your needle.

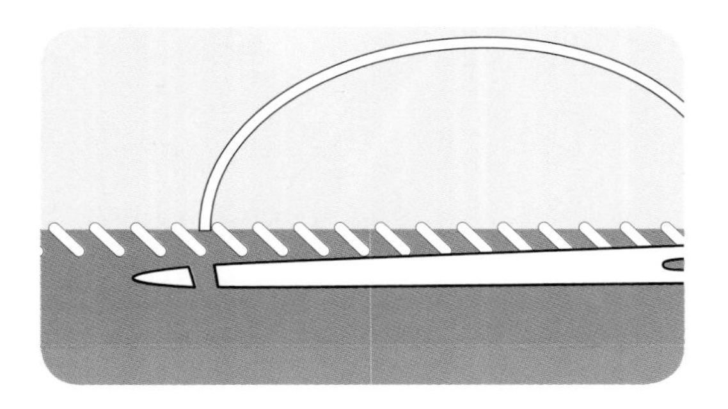

2 Wrap the working thread around the tip of the needle seven times. The working thread is the thread running from the fabric to the eye of the needle.

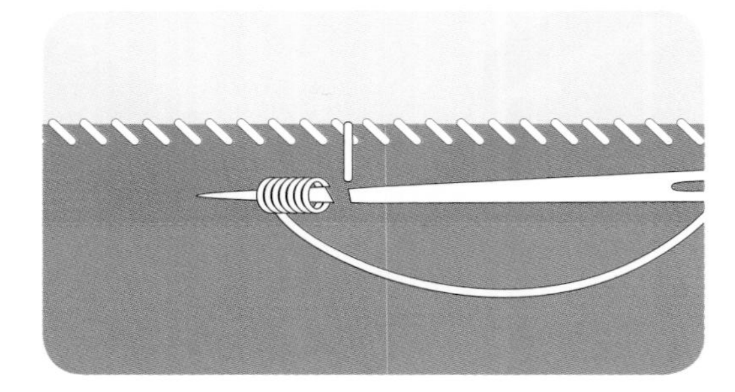

3 Pull the needle and thread through the wraps leaving a knot on the surface of the fabric. Make a small stitch to the left of the knot catching the background fabric and appliqué seam allowance only. Hold the working thread close to the background fabric and give it a gentle tug, "popping" the knot into the seam allowance. Pull up on the working thread and cut it close to the top of the fabric.

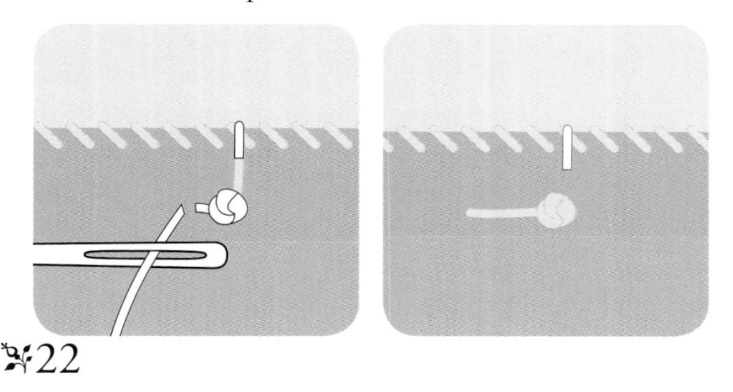

Beginning Again

As you appliqué, there will be times when you come to the end of the thread before you have finished stitching. When you reach the last 3" of thread, take the needle and thread to the back and end the stitching. To resume stitching, thread the needle and knot the thread referring to page 14 and follow these steps:

1 On the right side of your work, place the needle and knotted thread between the appliqué and background fabric, beginning several stitches back from where you ended the stitching. Bring the needle and thread to the front, one stitch away from the last stitch.

2 Continue appliquéing.

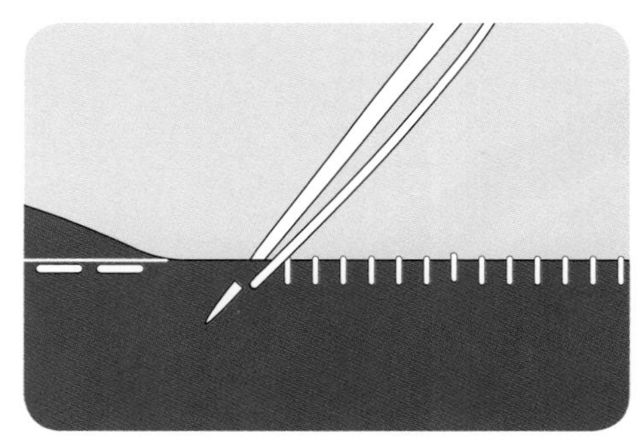

Tip *At some point during your appliqué journey, your thread may break unexpectedly. Don't worry, appliqué stitches are quite secure. Thread your needle with a new length of thread and knot. Beginning 4 to 5 stitches back from the point of the thread breaking, run the needle and thread between the appliqué and background fabrics. Appliqué over the last 4-5 stitches, then continue stitching as though the thread never broke.*

Reverse Appliqué

When the A was trimmed in prepartion for appliquéing it to the background fabric (page 12), the triangle in the center of the A was not trimmed. This was to prevent the fabric from fraying while the outer edges of the A were appliquéd. The inside triangle will be stitched using reverse appliqué. Reverse appliqué reveals the background fabric under the appliqué fabric, instead of covering the background fabric with the appliqué fabric as you have been doing to this point.

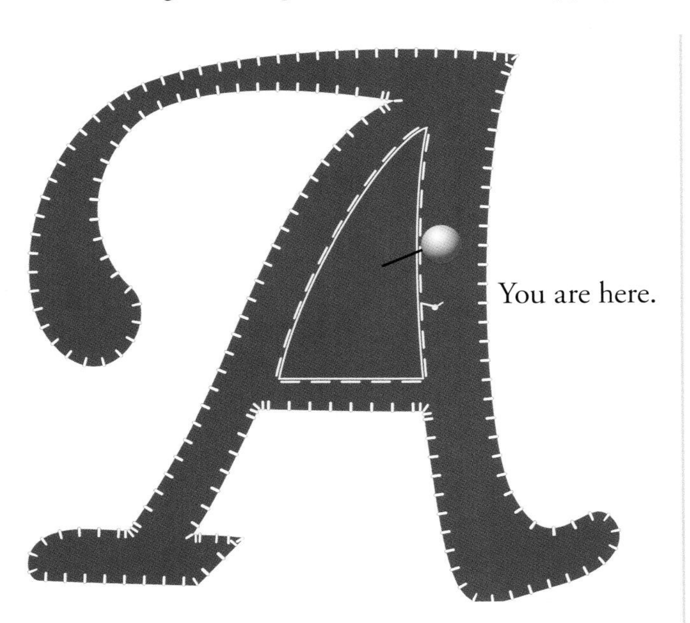

1 To trim the inside triangle, pinch the appliquè fabric upward with one hand and pinch the background fabric downward with your other hand. When you are sure the appliqué fabric is separated from the background fabric, cut a small slit in the appliqué fabric in the center of the triangle. Trim the inside of the triangle appliqué fabric only, leaving a 3/16" seam allowance from the drawn line.

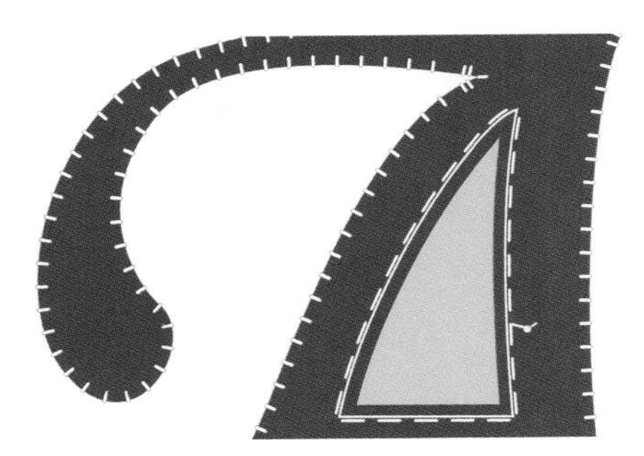

2 You are now ready to reverse appliqué the center triangle. At the middle of the triangle on the right hand side, begin appliquéing down to the inside bottom right corner.

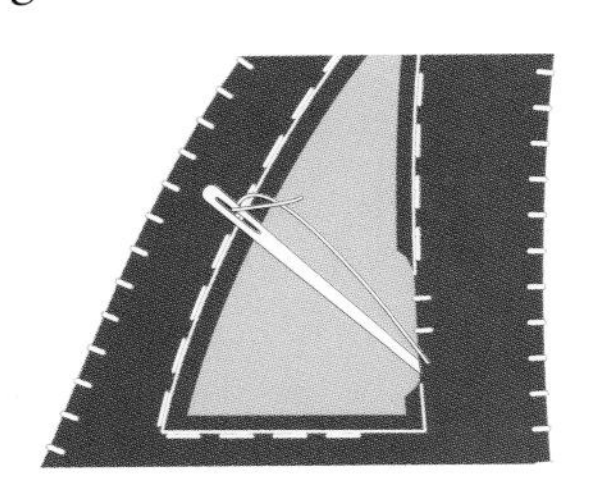

3 Appliqué across the bottom to the left inside corner.

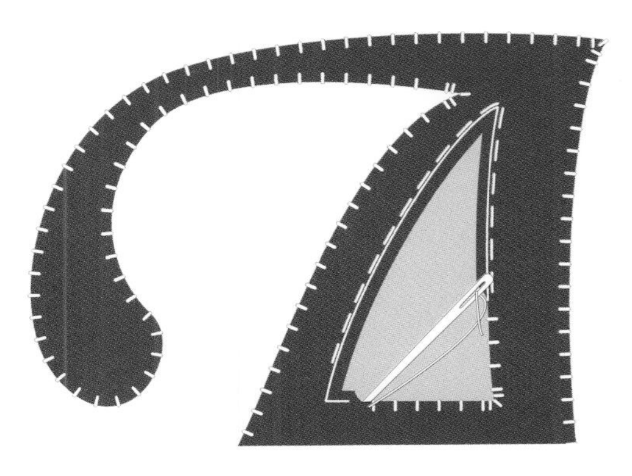

4 Appliqué up to the top inside corner of the triangle.

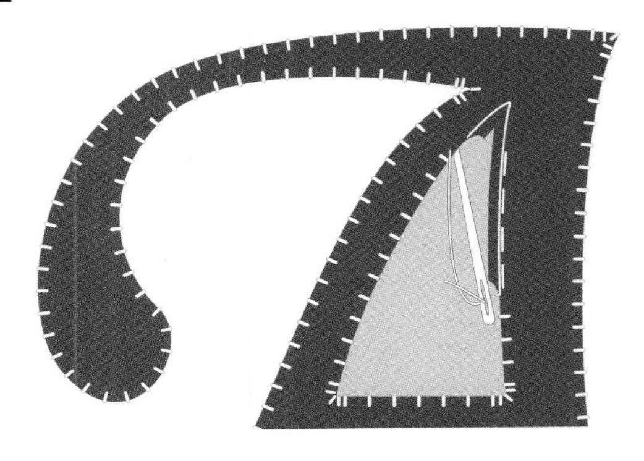

5 Appliqué down to the starting point, ending the stitching as described on page 22.

Congratulations on your first appliquéd letter.

Wreath Appliqué & Embellishment

The A is beautifully appliquéd and the wreath is ready to be eloquently embellished. You will begin by appliquéing the wreath stem following the basic instructions for preparing the appliqué fabric on page 12.

The Wreath

1 Cut a 7" x 7" piece of appliqué fabric for the wreath stem. On the wrong side of the background fabric, baste the wreath stem and background fabrics together along the drawn line. Baste the entire wreath stem, indicated on the pattern with the dotted lines through the flowers. Be sure to extend both ends of the stem into the circles at the top and the leaf at the bottom.

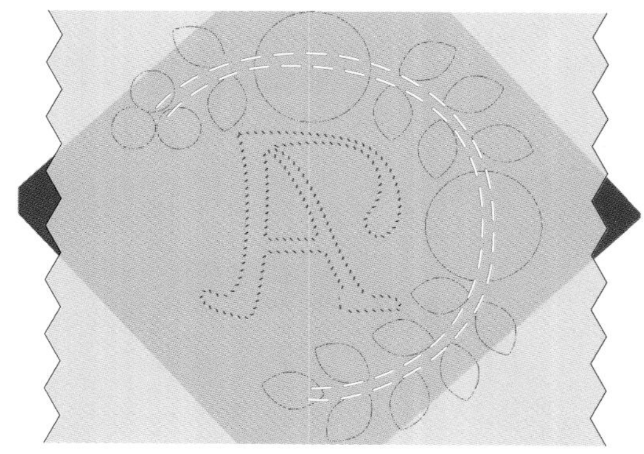

2 On the right side of the wreath stem fabric, mark around the outside edge of the basting stitches. Trim the 3⁄16" seam allowance on the appliqué fabric only.

3 Appliqué the wreath stem, referring to page 15. Do not appliqué the ends of the stem, which will be covered with a leaf or circles. Also, the gentle inside curve of the wreath stem will needleturn without requiring you to clip the seam allowance.

Padded Circles

Appliquéing a circle is simply stitching a continuous outside curve (page 18). Appliqué the seam allowance a short distance at a time and keep the stitches close together. Appliquéing circles can be a bit tricky at first, but as with all appliqué, practice will achieve beautiful results.

1 This method of padding circles requires the circle markings to be transferred to the right side of the background fabric. Baste around each circle drawn on the wrong side of the background fabric.

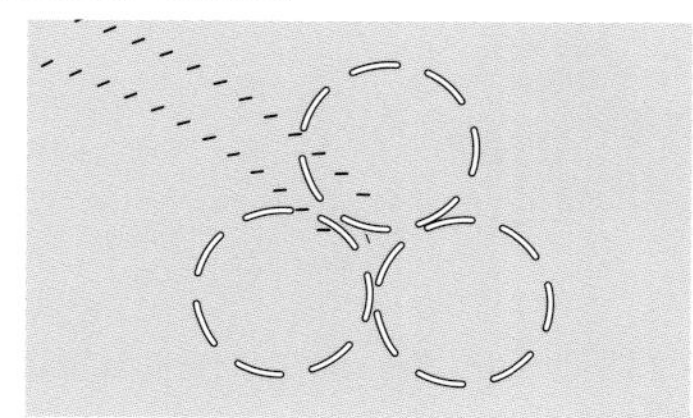

2 Using a circle template, cut a 5⁄8" circle from a piece of batting. Dab the circle of batting with a glue stick and center in one of the basted circles on the right side of the fabric. Cut a 7⁄8" circle from the appliqué fabric. Dab the wrong side of the circle with a glue stick and center over the batting circle.

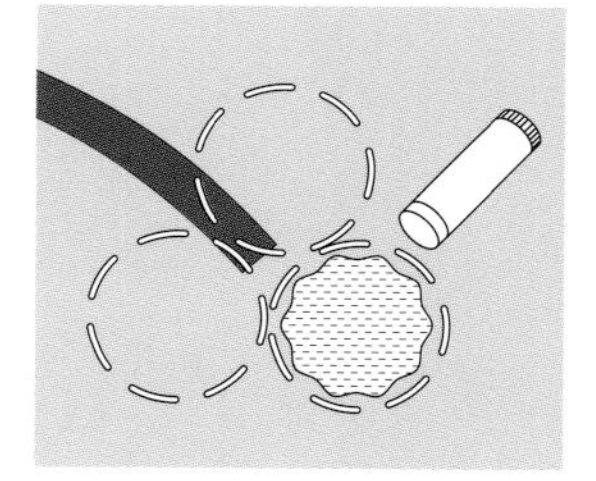

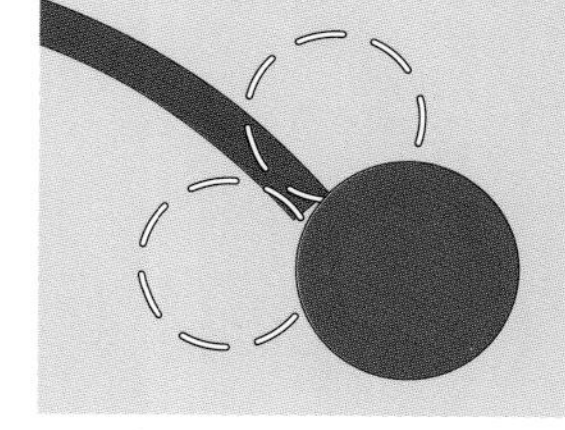

3 Appliqué the fabric circle around the edges of the batting and within the basted circle. Repeat for the remaining two circles. Remove the basting stitches.

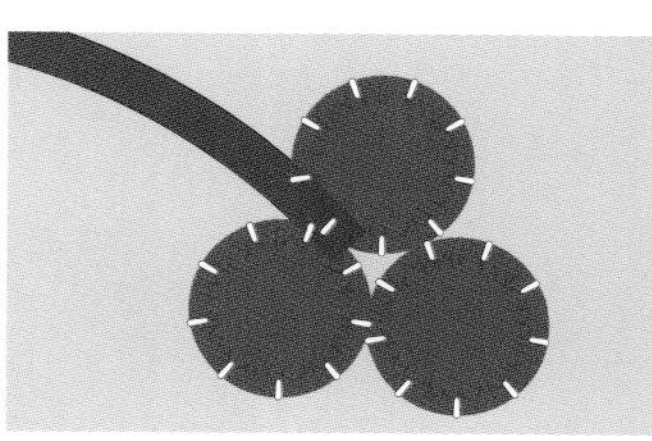

Refer to "The Art of Elegant Hand Embroidery, Embellishment and Appliqué" by Janice Vaine for additional circle techniques.

The Leaves

You are now ready to add the leaves to your wreath. The Perfect Placement Appliqué method on page 12 will be used for preparing the leaves for appliqué, with the exception of the top two leaves next to the padded circles. These leaves will have a special touch of ribbon embroidery embellishment. The leaves to be appliquéd may be basted and trimmed at one time to speed the preparation of the fabric for appliqué.

1 Cut a 2" x 2" piece of leaf fabric. Place the leaf fabric right side down on a flat surface, with the corners of the fabric on a diagonal. Place the background fabric right side down on top of the leaf fabric, centering one of the top five leaves on the leaf fabric. Pin in place.

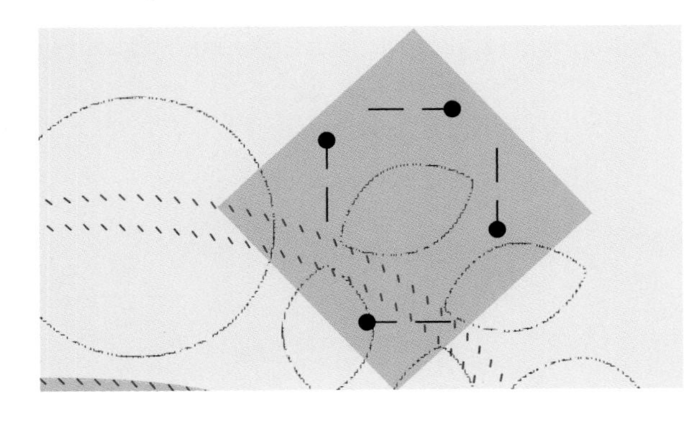

2 Thread a #9 Sharps needle with quilting thread in a color easily seen on the leaf fabric. Knot the end of the thread. With the wrong side of the background fabric facing up, baste the background and leaf fabric together along the drawn leaf.

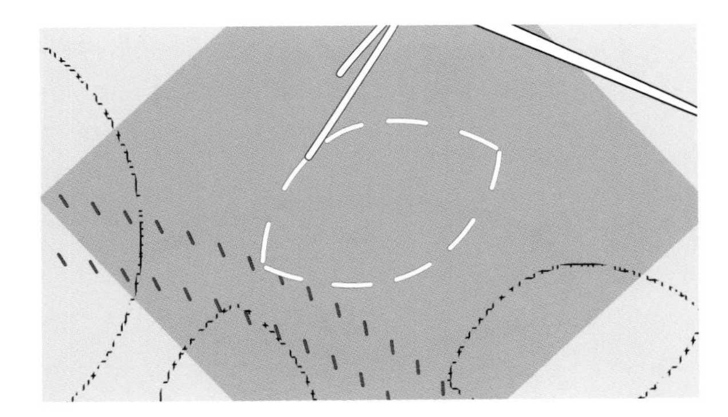

3 On the right side of the leaf fabric, use a marking pencil to trace next to the outside edge of the basting thread.

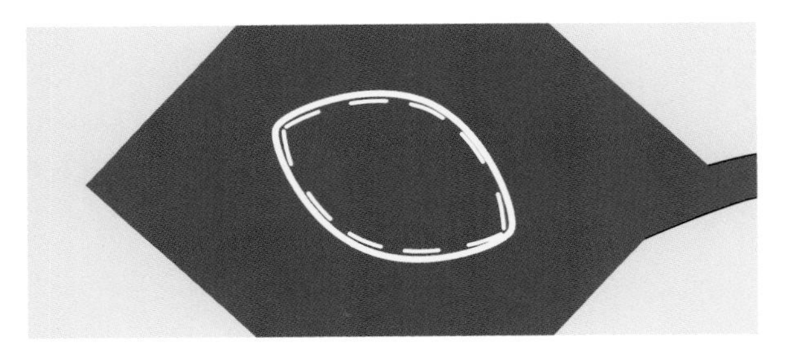

4 Trim the leaf fabric only, leaving a 3/16" seam allowance around the leaf.

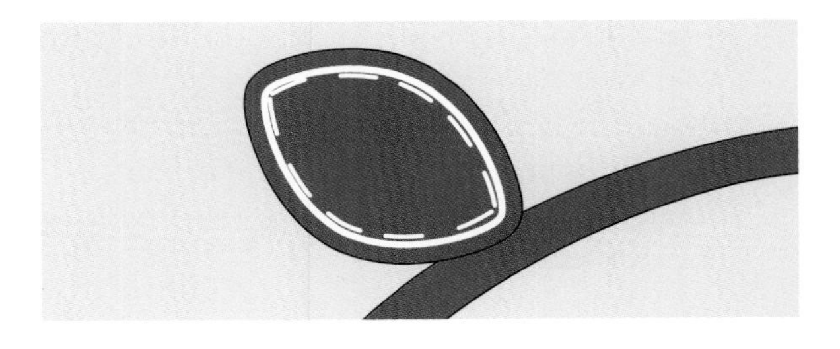

5 Repeat steps 1-4 for the remaining top four leaves and the bottom eight leaves.

6 Appliqué the leaves in place, referring to page 15.

A touch of embroidery adds interest to an appliquéd design. The next lesson will embellish your appliquéd leaves with an embroidered Stem Stitch vein down the center of each leaf.

Hooping

When adding embroidery to an appliqué block, it is best to select an embroidery hoop that will encompass the entire design. This alleviates the possibility of distorting or damaging the previously appliquéd and embroidered elements on the block. A 10" embroidery hoop will be used to add embellishment to the block.

There is a correct way to hoop fabric without distorting the grain of the fabric and thereby the design. Correct hooping will also ensure meticulous and beautiful stitch results. Use a quality hoop to maintain even fabric tension throughout stitching. Hoops that allow the fabric to puddle as you progress through the stitching will cause uneven and irregular stitches. An interlocking hoop, such as the Morgan No-Slip Hoop®, is a good choice.

1 Slightly loosen the screw on the outer ring. Loosen the screw just enough for the inner ring to be released.

2 Pop the rings apart.

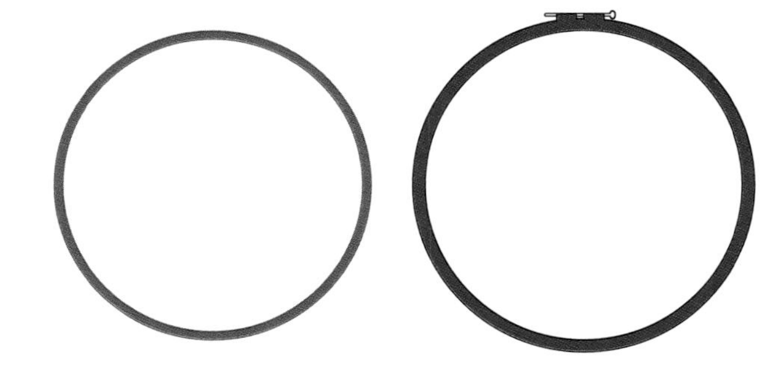

Tip *The elements of a design you choose to embroider should be marked on the right side of the fabric before hooping. For the A block, you may wish to mark the leave veins on each of the appliquéd leaves before hooping. The remaining two leaves to be embroidered should be marked following the instructions on* *page 29.*

3 Place the inner ring on a flat surface. Place the fabric on top of the inner ring with the design centered over the ring.

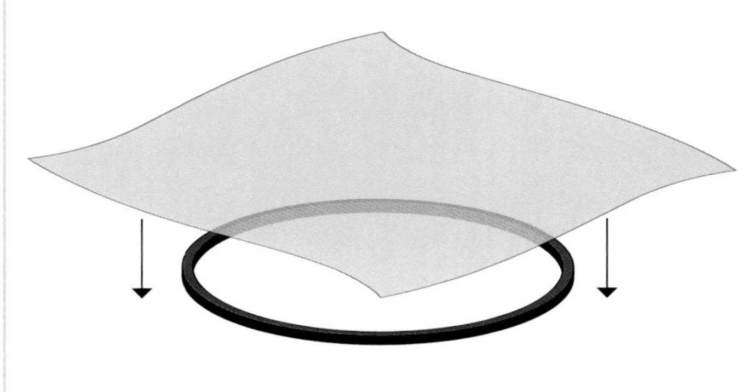

4 Fit the outer ring over the fabric onto the inner ring. It should pull the fabric taut and smooth. Do not pull the fabric to adjust, which may distort the design. If the fabric is not taut in the hoop, remove the outer ring and repeat the steps.

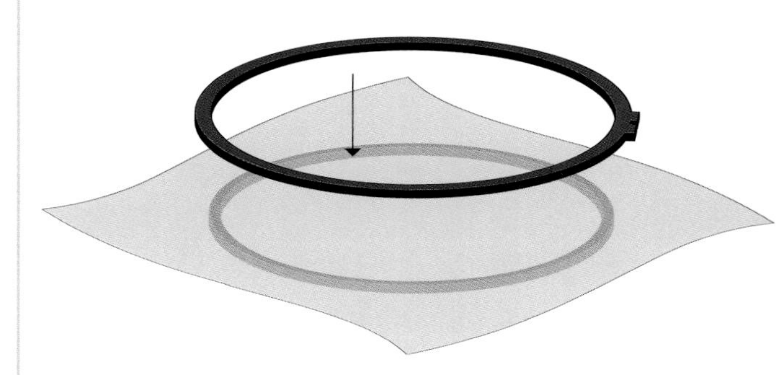

Tip *Always remove the fabric from the hoop at the end of each stitching session. Leaving the hoop on the fabric may permanently crease or mark the fabric.*

Separating or Pouncing Embroidery Threads

Embroidery flosses are the most commonly used threads for embroidery stitches. Flosses come in skeins consisting of multiple-ply cotton or silk threads. These threads must be separated before being placed in the eye of the needle and used for stitching. Even if the intent is to place all the strands or plies of the thread skein in the needle, the plies must be individually separated. This allows the strands to "fluff", resulting in better coverage on the fabric and a more luxurious stitch. The method of separating the threads is called stripping the threads and begins with pouncing.

1 Cut a length of thread no longer than 18". A good rule of thumb is a length from the tip of your forefinger to your elbow. This will alleviate fraying and thread breakage. Specialty threads, such as metallics, will benefit from being cut shorter.

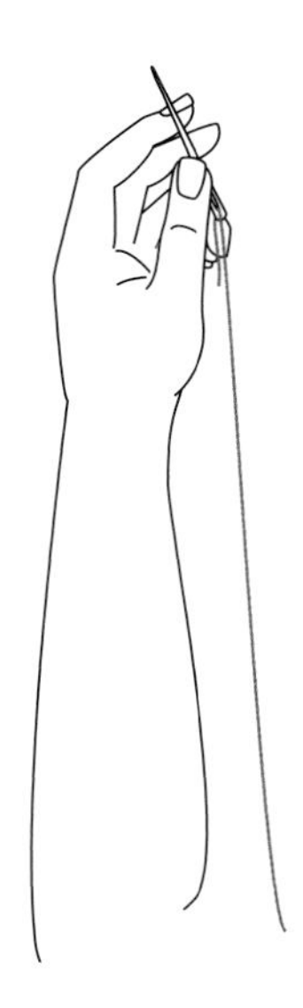

2 Pounce the end of the threads by lightly tapping the cut end with your forefinger. If the threads blossom apart, this will be the end to pull out the individual strands. If it does not blossom, try pouncing the other end.

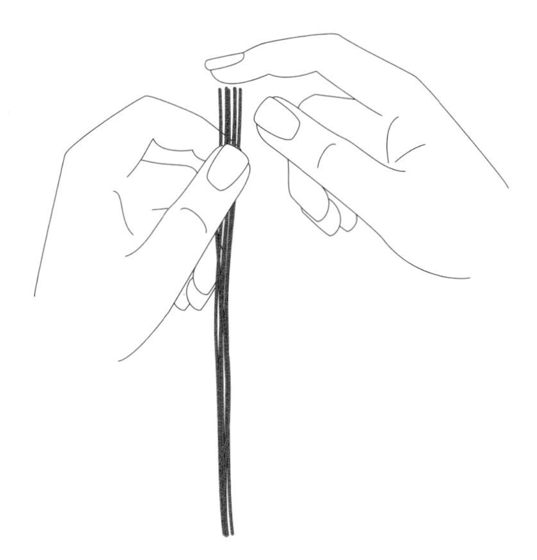

3 Holding the threads between your forefinger and thumb, 1" below the thread blossom, pull an individual thread up from among the others. The remaining threads will gather below your thumb and forefinger. Lay the individual thread on a flat surface. Repeat until all the plies have been stripped or separated. Lay the threads back together all in the same direction.

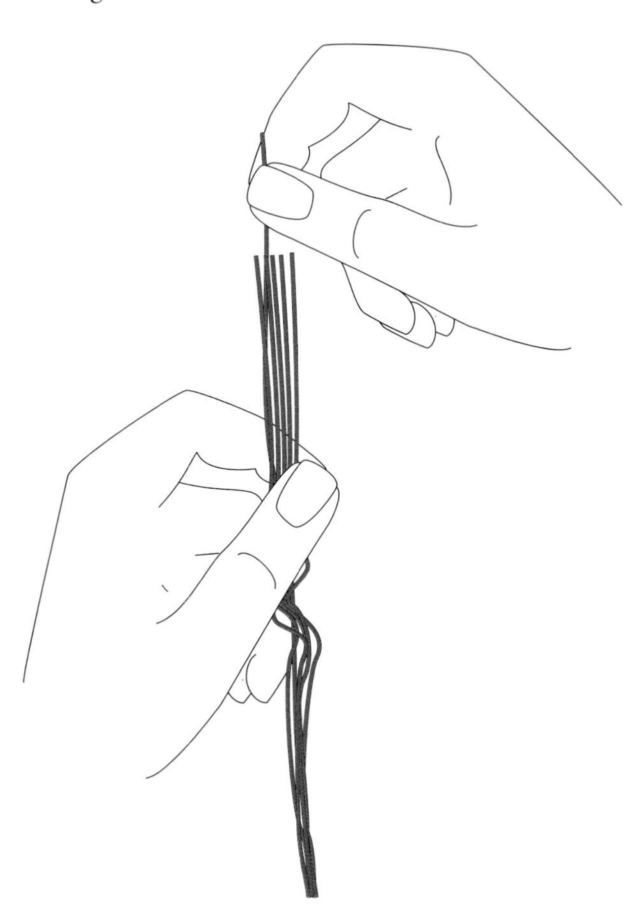

4 Rejoin the number of threads to be used for the selected embroidery stitch and thread the needle.

Stem Stitch Leaf Veins

Your block is in the hoop and you have stripped the embroidery floss. Thread a #9 Crewel needle with one strand of green floss.

1 If you have not yet done so, lightly mark a line down the center of each leaf, starting slightly below the tip of the leaf. Add side veins as desired.

2 Bring the needle and thread to the front at the top of the leaf at A. With the working thread below the needle (swings low), take the needle to the back at B and up at C, between A and B.

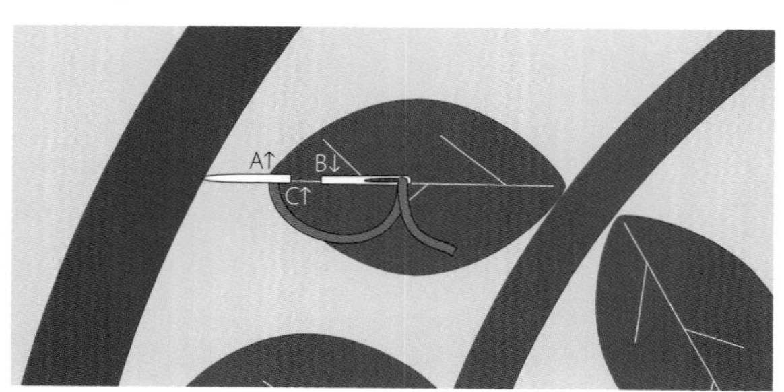

3 Pull the needle and thread through the fabric. Again with the working thread below the needle (swings low), take the needle down at D and up at B.

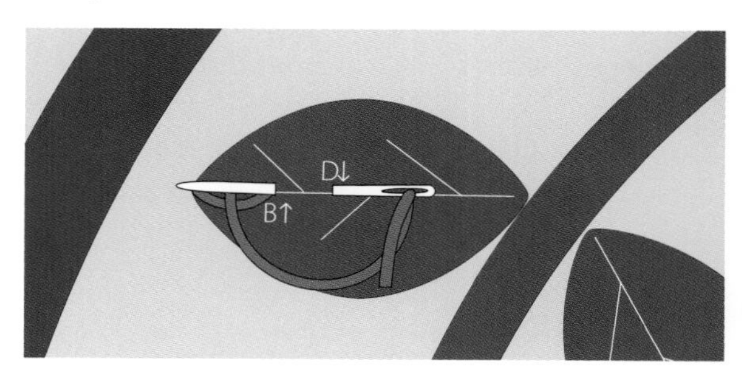

4 Following step 3 continue working stitches down to the bottom of the leaf. Always keep the thread below the needle. To end, take the thread to the back at E for the last stitch without re-emerging. Secure on the back. Stem stitch the side veins.

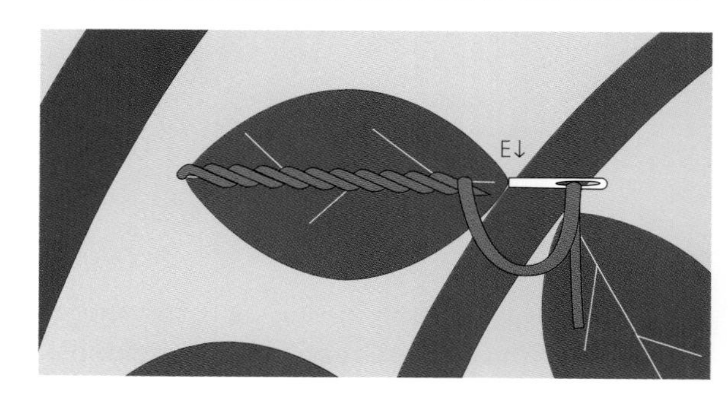

5 Repeat on all the appliquéd leaves. When finished, remove the block from the hoop.

Marking the Design for Embroidery

The two final leaves will be embroidered using the Fishbone Stitch and ribbon. Since the block has been appliquéd using the Perfect Placement Appliqué method, you need to transfer the markings for the remaining leaves from the wrong side to the right side of the background fabric. The block should be out of the hoop.

1 On the wrong side of the background fabric, baste along the traced lines of the remaining two leaves.

2 On the right side of the background fabric, lightly trace along the outside edge of the basting stitches on both leaves. Draw a line down the center of each leaf.

3 Remove the basting stitches.

Tip *Another option for transferring the design from the back to the front is to place the block on a light box right side up and trace the two remaining leaves onto the right side of the background fabric.*

Threading & Knotting Silk Ribbon

The remaining two leaves will be worked with silk ribbon and the Fishbone Stitch. Intermingling and nestling silk ribbon embroidery within an appliqué design has eye-catching appeal. Here are the basics you will need for successful ribbon embroidery.

Threading the Needle with Ribbon

1 Cut a 12" length of green 4mm silk ribbon, cutting the end of the ribbon diagonally. Always use short lengths of ribbon, no longer than 12", to prevent fraying and damage to the ribbon.

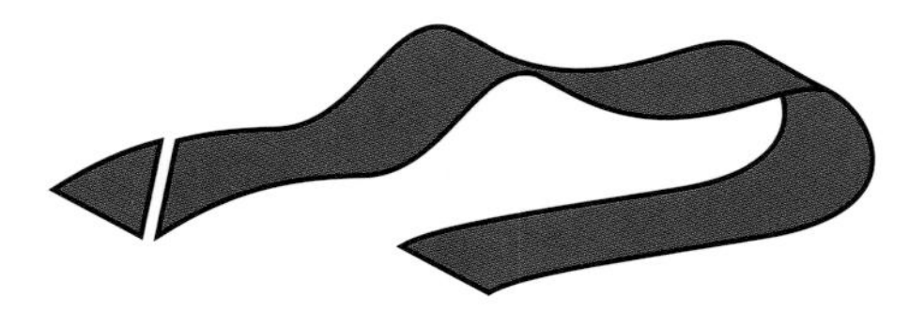

2 Press the ribbon using the iron's silk setting. Holding the iron flat, pull the ribbon under the iron to press.

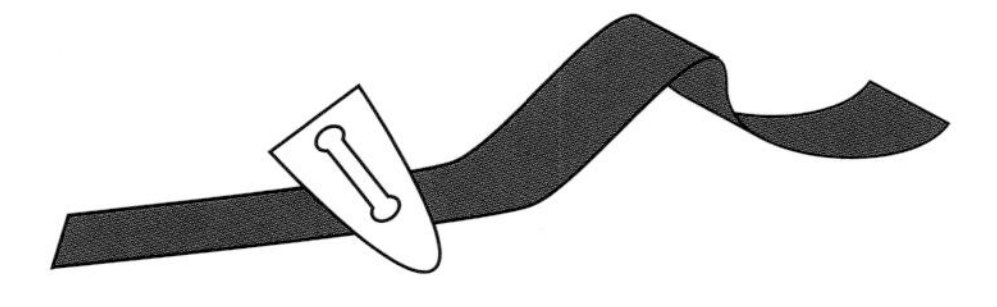

3 Thread the diagonally cut end of the silk ribbon through the eye of a #22 Chenille needle, sliding the needle along the ribbon approximately 2".

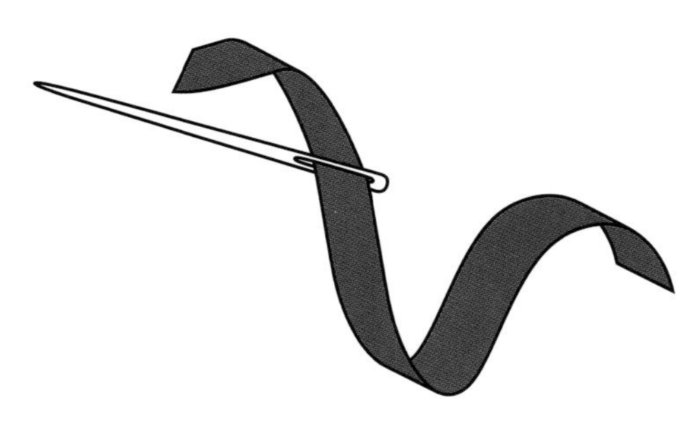

4 Place the point of the needle ¼" from the diagonal cut end of the ribbon. Push the needle through the ribbon up to the eye of the needle.

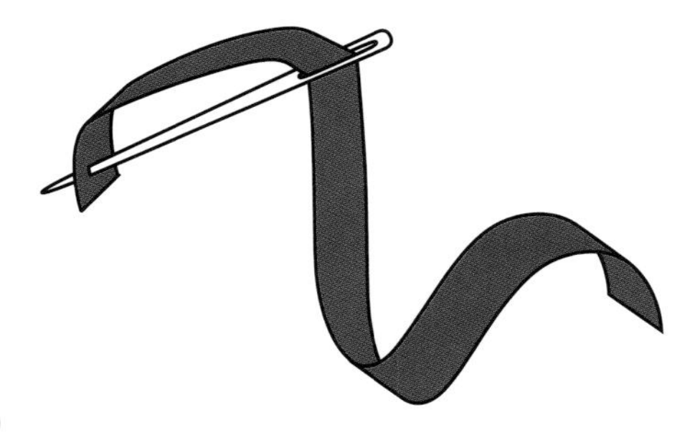

5 Hold the tail of the ribbon in one hand and pull the needle with the other hand until a knot forms at the eye of the needle. This will keep the slick silk ribbon from coming out of the eye of the needle while you are stitching. It will easily pass through the fabric as you stitch.

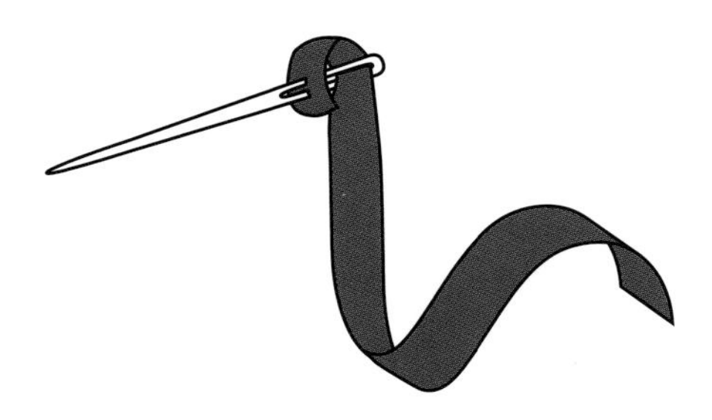

Knotting the Ribbon

1 Take the opposite end of the ribbon and turn back a ¼" tab. Place the ¼" tab and the working ribbon onto the tip of the needle.

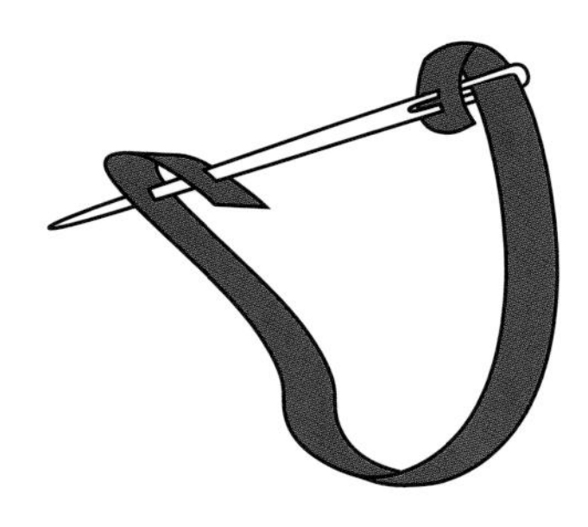

2 Pull the needle and ribbon through the tab. Push the tab to the end of the ribbon to form a delicate knot.

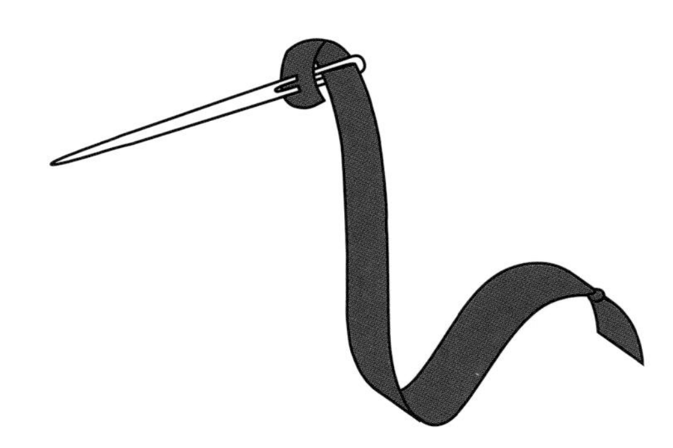

Fishbone Stitch Leaves

The Fishbone Stitch is one of my favorite stitches. It makes beautiful leaves in threads and ribbon, from tiny little leaves with one strand of floss to larger leaves with 13mm silk ribbon. Center your block in a 10" embroidery hoop to add these delicate ribbonwork stitches.

1 Bring the needle and ribbon to the front at A. Take the needle from B to C. Make sure the ribbon is to the right of the needle.

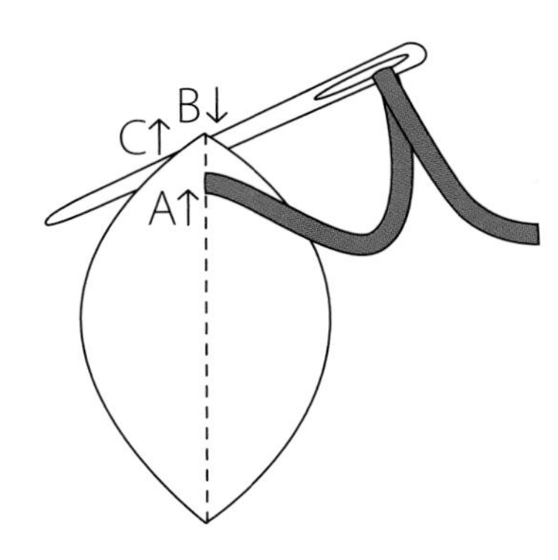

2 Pull the needle and ribbon through the fabric. Make sure the ribbon is to the left of the needle. Take the needle from D to E.

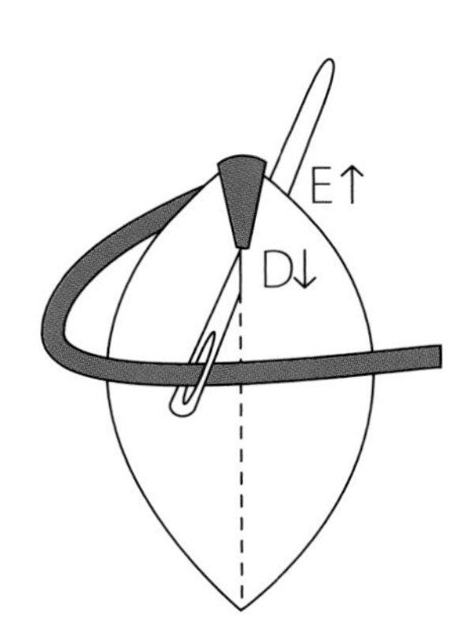

3 Pull the needle and ribbon through the fabric. Make sure the ribbon is to the right of the needle. Take the needle from F to G.

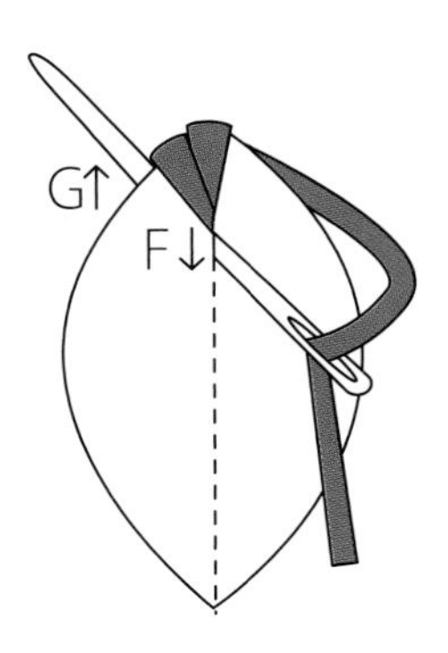

4 Pull the needle and ribbon through the fabric. Continue working down the leaf from side to side following steps 2-3.

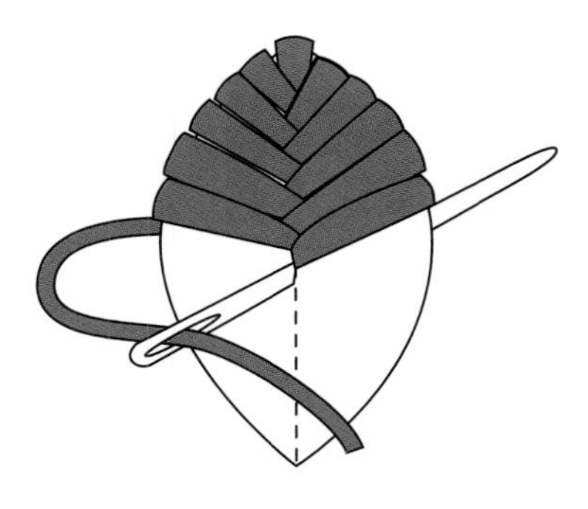

5 Finish the stitching by taking the needle and ribbon to the back at the bottom of the center line at H.

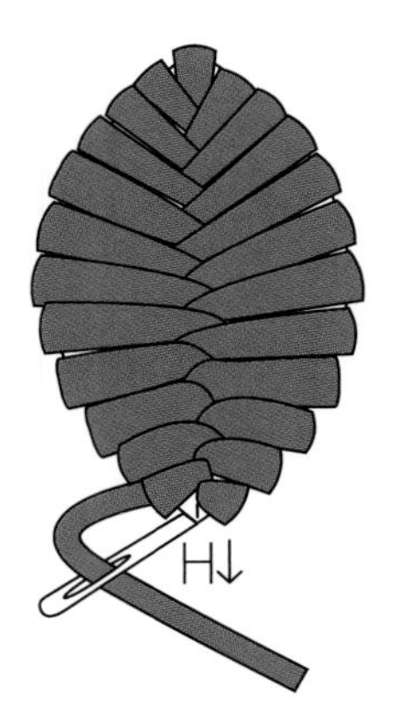

6 Using a separate needle and thread, secure the ribbon to the back with several straight stitches. Be sure the stitches do not show through to the front.

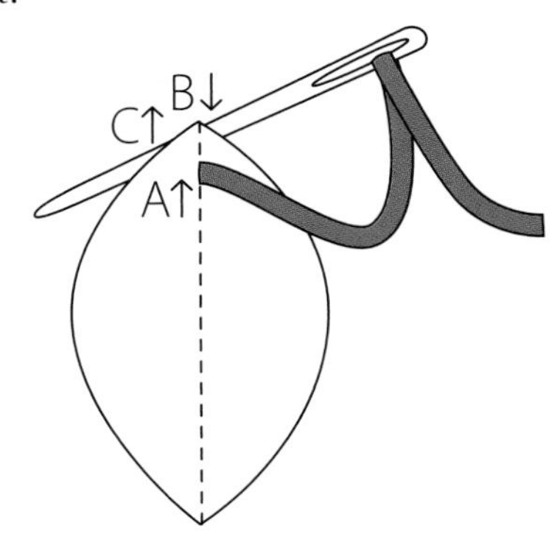

Jan's Ruched Rose

Ruched flowers are made with a strip of fabric or ribbon gathered on a gathering thread that has been stitched in a repeat pattern. As the gathering thread is pulled, the strip forms scallops or petals. Jan's Ruched Rose is made to blossom from smaller to larger petals as the flower is worked from the center to the outside edge, blossoming as you stitch. It will add an exquisite finishing touch to your A block.

1 Cut a strip of fabric 1¼" by 33". Fold both lengthwise edges toward the center, wrong sides together, and press. The finished width of the strip is ⅝".

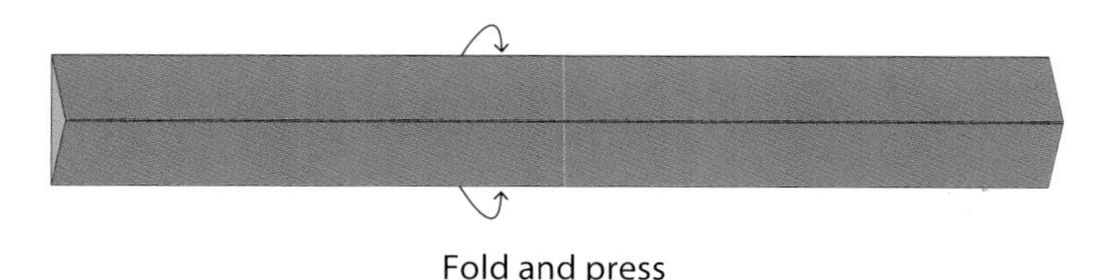

Fold and press

2 Working on the front side of the fabric strip, mark dots on the top and bottom folds as indicated.

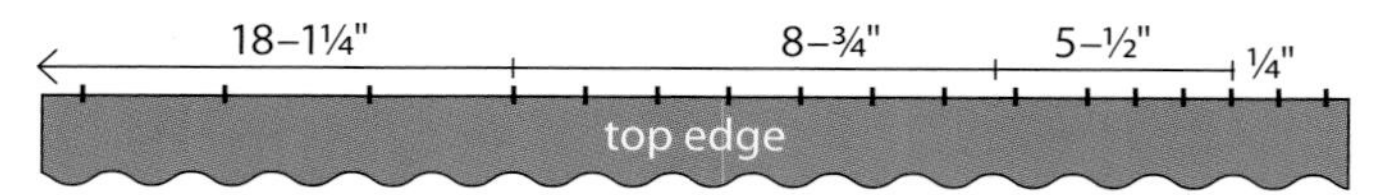

Place a dot ¼" from the top right edge.
From the dot: mark 5–½" increments
mark 8–¾" increments
mark 18–1¼" increments

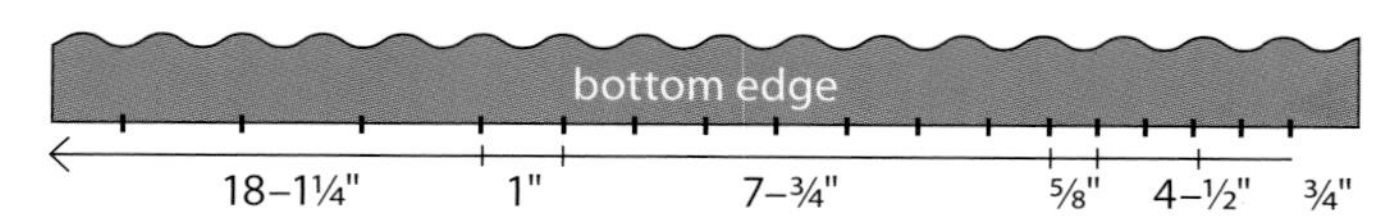

Place a dot ¾" from the bottom right edge.
From the dot: mark 4–½" increments
mark 1–⅝" increment
mark 7–¾" increments
mark 1–1" increment
mark 18–1¼" increments.

Trim the left edge of the fabric or ribbon ¼" from the last marked dot on the bottom edge.

3 Double thread a #10 Sharps needle and 50 wt. cotton thread in a color matching the fabric. Knot the end of the thread. Using the marked dots as a guide for stitching a "V" pattern, bring the needle to the front at A, and stitch down to B, stitch up to C, stitch down to D, and so on until five mountain tops are stitched.

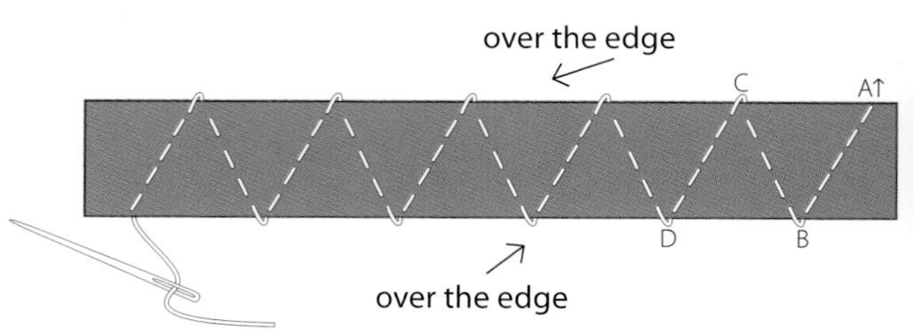

4 Gently gather the fabric on the stitches forming petals. Once gathered, the stitching line will run through the center of the fabric, with petals on the top and bottom of the stitching line. Knot the thread to secure the gathers.

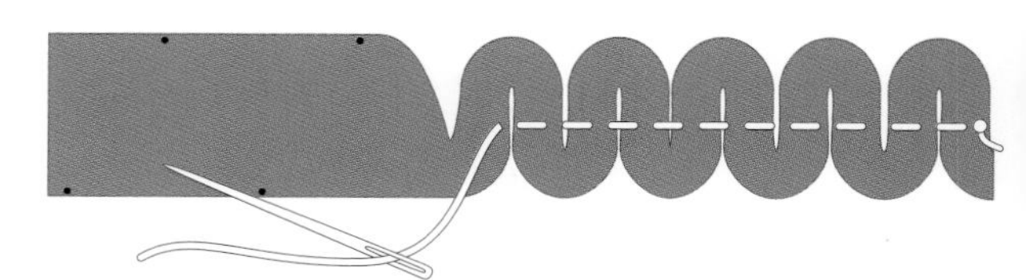

5 Work four more mountain tops, gather and knot and repeat. As a general rule, the width of a petal should be the size of a pinky fingernail once gathered.
As you work along the strip gathering the petals, you will begin to notice the petals gradually getting larger and fuller. Continue gathering the length of the strip working four mountain tops at a time and knotting. By knotting after stitching and gathering, if the gathered thread should break, you will not have to restitch the entire length of the strip.

Jan's Ruched Rose *continued*

6 Rethread the needle with a new double length of thread. Bring the needle from the back to the front in the first five bottom petals.

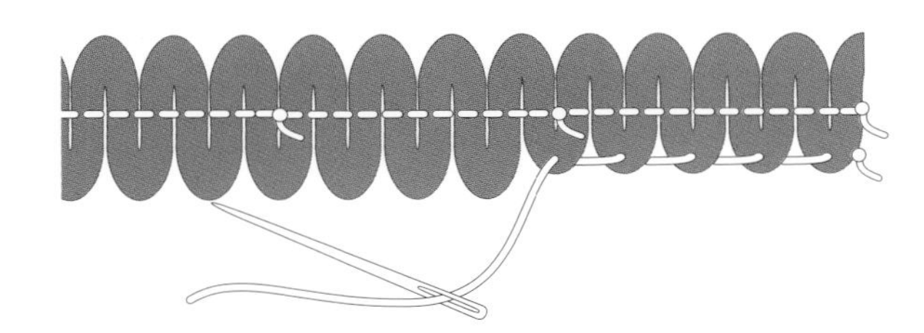

7 Pull the working thread and gather, forming the flower center. Knot to secure the gathers. Place the first and fifth petals right sides together. Wrap the working thread tightly several times between the petals. Secure. Open the five petals flat revealing the flower center. DO NOT CUT the thread after knotting.

8 Continue to wrap the petals around and behind the flower center, trying to offset the mountain tops. Every two to three petals, secure the petals to the previous round of petals with tiny stitches, hiding the stitches in the folds of the gathered petals.

9 Continue working the petals around the flower to the desired finished size. Angle the end of the fabric to the back of the flower and secure.

10 Position the flower on the wreath. Secure to the block with tiny stitches hidden in the folds of the gathered petals. Repeat for the second rose.

And there you have it, your first appliquéd and embellished block!

Pressing and Trimming Blocks

Once your blocks are appliquéd and embellished, they need to be pressed and trimmed to size.

Pressing the Block

1. Triple fold a thick terry cloth towel. Pressing your block on a terry cloth towel will help retain the fullness of your appliqué and embellishments and not flatten them out.

2. Place the embellished block RIGHT SIDE DOWN on the towel. Lightly mist with Mary Ellen's Best Press™ and press with a dry iron. DO NOT use steam.

Note: *If you have used threads, ribbons, or any fibers that are not colorfast, do not use any liquids when pressing, including steam.*

Trimming the Block

1. Center a 9½" x 9½" ruler over the appliquéd embellished block. Make note if the pattern calls for the block to be square or set on point. In the pillow project, the block is set on point. Lightly trace around the outside edge of the ruler, marking the block to size.

Squared

On point

Note: *If the finished size of one block is different, center and trace the finished block size, plus seam allowances, around the outside edge of the block.*

2. Because of the raised embellishment, it may not have been possible to trace a perfect square. Therefore, place the block on a rotary cutting mat. With a 6½" x 12½" ruler and rotary cutter and using the traced markings as a guide, trim the block to the desired size.

"A" is for Appliqué Pillow

Pillow is 16" x 16" finished.

by Janice Vaine, Jacksonville, FL

Fabric Requirements

Appliquéd and embellished "A" block
Setting triangles . . . . .Fat quarter*
Binding. . . . . .Fat quarter*
Backing. . . . . .Fat quarter*
Pillow form. . . . . .15"
Lace . . . . .1½ yards
*Fat quarter is 18" x 22".

Cutting

Setting triangles:
2–11" x 11" squares
cut in half once diagonally

Backing:
1–16½" x 16½" square

Binding:
4–3⅛" x 22" strips
sew end to end and press in half lengthwise wrong sides together

"A" is for Appliqué Pillow *continued*

Pillow construction

1 Trim your embellished block to measure 9½" x 9½" *on point.*

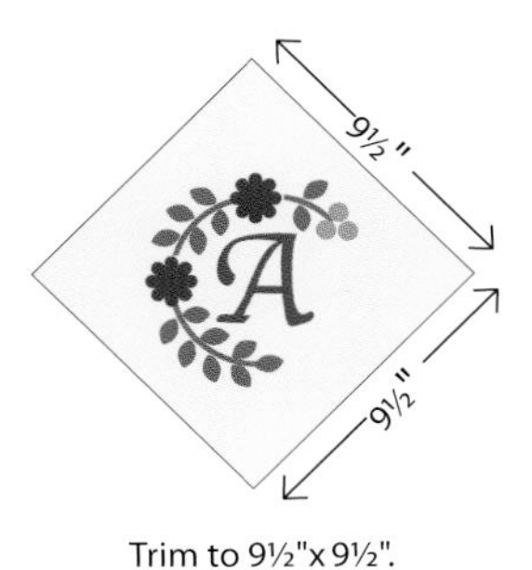

Trim to 9½"x 9½".

2 Use ¼" seam allowances unless otherwise indicated. Sew the setting triangles to the appliqué block. Trim to 16½" x 16½" square.

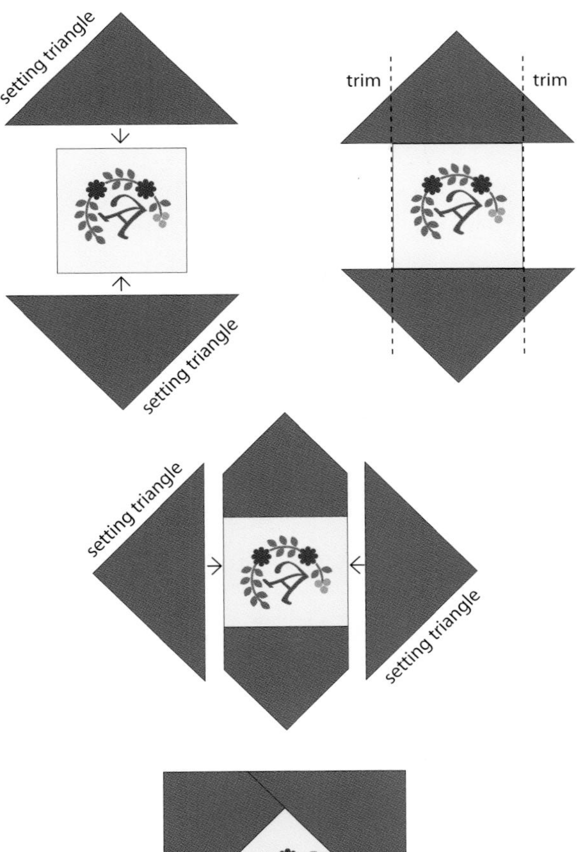

Trim to 16½" x 16½".

3 Beginning in a corner, pin lace around the edge of the center block, mitering or gathering corners as desired. Sew lace to the block with a tiny zigzag stitch, setting sewing machine to stitch width 1, stitch length 1.

4 Place the pillow front and backing wrong sides together. Baste together leaving a 10" opening. Sew double-fold binding around the basted edged of the pillow front with a ½" seam allowance. Leave the 10" opening on bottom edge. Insert pillow form. Sew opening close. Finish attaching the binding.

pillow back

10" opening

10" opening

Pillow is 16" x 16" finished.

Alphabet Sampler, 89" x 89"
by Janice Vaine and Gena Holland; quilted by Marilyn Lange

Alphabet

the blocks

This chapter features the letters of the alphabet artistically encircled by a floral wreath. Each letter is an opportunity to learn and perfect your hand appliqué skills, while the wreaths present a creative skill-builder as you learn new embroidery and embellishing techniques.

Each wreath and letter includes close-up photography of the stitched block, a chart outlining the stitching order and techniques used, and the supplies needed to create the stitches. The suggested stitches and techniques can be found on the pages listed in the chart. Tips are included to ensure your success and a full-size block pattern is located on the facing page.

As you gain confidence in your skills, you may wish to mix and match letters and wreaths. Choose your favorite combination and use it in one of the projects beginning on page 117 or design your own creation. The possibilities are limited only by your imagination.

Follow these simple instructions to combine various letters and wreaths:

1. Make a photocopy of the letter and wreath blocks you wish to combine.
2. Using a light box, center and trace the letter onto an 8½" x 11" sheet of paper.
3. Place the photocopy of the wreath under the traced letter, centering the letter in the wreath.
4. Place both on the light box and trace the wreath around the letter.

Please note not all the letters will fit into all the wreaths. There is an enlargement and reduction chart on page 126 if you wish to resize one of the patterns. The photocopying of block patterns is for individual personal use only.

Notice too the quotes on the bottom of each pattern page. They are there to provide encouragement and inspiration throughout your stitching journey. They include thoughts on creativity, discovery, patience, perseverance and relaxation. Each is as essential as the stitching skills you are learning.

the letter A

The letter A is a perfect lesson in needleturn appliqué techniques, while the wreath offers simple lessons in embroidered embellishment. Marry the two and you are primed for success as you begin your stitching journey.

In Gena's block, different stitches and techniques were chosen rather than those taught In the Classroom with Jan. It illustrates the opportunity for individual creativity within each block.

"A" by Gena Holland, Anderson, SC

Tip

When working the Raised Stem Stitch, be certain the foundation stitches are laying on the surface of the fabric without pulling it. When weaving the Stem Stitches, be careful to keep the outline even. Avoid pulling the stitches too tightly and distorting the shape of the wreath.

	Stitch/Technique	page #	Fabric/Thread/Ribbon
1	Letter A – Appliqué	10-23	12" square of background fabric 6" square of fabric for letter
2	Wreath Stem– Raised Stem Stitch	106	2 strands of 6-stranded cotton floss Gentle Art #0440 Maple Syrup
3	Leaves – Boat Leaf	94	Five each ⅝" x 3½" pieces of French Ombré Wired Ribbon #48-9, #49-7, and #49-12
4	Large Flowers – Gathered Flowers	99	One 1" x 24" piece French Ombré Wired Ribbon #48-3 for each flower
	Flower Centers – Traveler's Joy and Colonial Knot	114 97	1" circle for single Traveler's Joy 3 strands of 6-stranded cotton floss Gentle Art #7020 Butternut Squash
5	Small Flowers – Traveler's Joy	114	Bottom petals of each flower made with a 2¼" circle Top petals of each flower made with a 1½" circle
	Small Flower Centers – Colonial Knot	97	3 strands of 6-stranded cotton floss Gentle Art #1120 Cherry Bark

"She watched and taught the girls that sang at their embroidery frames while the great silk flowers grew from their needles."
~Louise Jordan Miln~
The Feast of Lanterns

the letter B

The techniques used in the B wreath combine embroidery with appliqué. Notice how the embroidered Fishbone Stitch leaves blend subtly with the appliquéd leaves.

The grouping of Gathered Flowers reminds me of a hydrangea. The ribbon has a light edge and a dark edge, offering two different flower values. It makes this blossom come to life in color and dimension.

"B" by Janice Vaine, Jacksonville, FL

Tip

The Gathered Flower is versatile, fun to experiment with and easy to make. Try different ribbons in various widths and lengths, fabrics from soft chiffons and silks to cottons and batiks. What will bloom as you gather and stitch?

	Stitch/Technique	page #	Fabric/Thread/Ribbon
1	Letter B – Appliqué	10-23	12" square of background fabric 6" square of fabric for letter
2	Wreath Stem – Appliqué	24	7" square of fabric
3	10 Bottom Leaves – Appliqué	25	Ten 2" squares of fabric for leaves on left and right of center flower
	Appliquéd Leaf Veins – Stem Stitch	112	1 strand of 6-stranded cotton floss Gentle Art #0130 Avocado
	Side Veins – Straight Stitch	113	1 strand of 6-stranded cotton floss Gentle Art #0130 Avocado
4	6 Top Leaves – Fishbone Stitch	98	1 strand of Gentle Art Simply Wool #0130-W Avocado
5	Flower – Gathered Flowers	99	One ½" x 4½" piece of French Ribbon Variation #0035-2 for each flower; make 7
	Flower Centers – Beads	93	3 beads each flower Mill Hill Frosted Glass Beads #62041

"Kindred spirits are not as scarce as I used to think.
It's splendid to find out there are so many of them in the world."
~L.M. Montgomery~
Anne of Green Gables

the letter C

This block shows how some of the techniques within the book may be done in miniature. The flower centers in the middle of each Petal Flower is a tiny Traveler's Joy. Don't you love the daintiness of the little flower within a flower?

The single Traveler's Joy was made with a 1" circle. Can you envision this little flower made in multiples of soft purples to form a lilac?

"C" by Gena Holland, Anderson, SC

	Stitch/Technique	page #	Fabric/Thread/Ribbon
1	Letter C – Appliqué	10-23	12" square of background fabric 6" square of fabric for letter
2	Wreath Stem – Appliqué	24	8" square of fabric
3	Leaves – Appliqué	25	Twenty 2" squares of fabric
	Appliquéd Leaf Veins – Stem Stitch	112	1 strand of 6-stranded cotton floss Gentle Art #7041 Apple Cider
4	Flowers – Petal Flower	104	Four 2½" fabric circles for each flower (8 back petals) Four 2" fabric circles for each flower (8 top petals)
	Flower Centers – Traveler's Joy and Colonial Knot	114 97	Four 1½" fabric circles for single Traveler's Joy 3 strands of 6-stranded cotton floss Gentle Art #7020 Butternut Squash

Tip

Try forming the Petal Flower on a square of crinoline instead of the muslin. Crinoline provides a stable foundation on which to work dimensional flowers, so there is no need to hoop it. Simply trim the excess crinoline from behind the flower when finished stitching and attach the flower to your block.

"Don't let the fear of the time it will take to accomplish something stand in your way of doing it. The time will pass anyway; we might just as well put that passing time to the best possible use."
~Earl Nightingale~

the letter D

"Mistakes are the portals of discovery."
James Joyce, Irish author (1882-1941)

And so Jan's Ruched Rose was formed. While teaching a class, a student inadvertently marked her ruching segments too wide. Instead of redoing the whole strip, we decided to see what would happen. It made a beautiful large petalled flower.

I continued to experiment with varying the width of segments from small to large, and this hybrid flower bloomed.

"D" by Janice Vaine, Jacksonville, FL

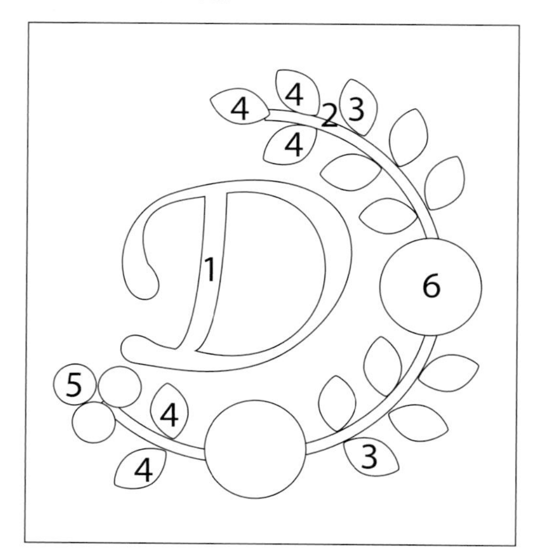

 Tip

The little flowers on this block were made by ruching only the five center petals of Jan's Ruched Rose. These tiny flowers make beautiful centers on other flowers too.

You may try removing the top and bottom wires for softer flower petals.

	Stitch/Technique	page #	Fabric/Thread/Ribbon
1	Letter D – Appliqué	10-23	12" square of background fabric 6" square of fabric for letter
2	Wreath Stem – Appliqué	24	7" square of fabric
3	10 Middle Leaves – Appliqué	25	Ten 2" squares of fabric for leaves on top and bottom of right flower
	Appliquéd Leaf Veins – Stem Stitch	112	1 strand of 6-stranded cotton floss Gentle Art #0112 Grasshopper
	Side Veins – Straight Stitch	113	1 strand of 6-stranded cotton floss Gentle Art #7080 Endive
4	5 Leaves at Tips of the Wreath – Fishbone Stitch	98	3 strands of 6-stranded cotton floss Gentle Art #0112 Grasshopper Gentle Art #7080 Endive
5	Small Flowers – Jan's Ruched Rose	100	One ⅝" x 4⅝" piece French Ombré Wired Ribbon #11100-828 and two pieces #11194-140 for the three small flowers; remove bottom wire; form the 5 center petals of Jan's Ruched Rose; make 3
	Small Flower Centers – Beads	93	3 beads for each flower Mill Hill Antique Glass Beads #03046
6	Large Flowers – Jan's Ruched Rose	100	One each ⅝" x 33" piece of French Ombré Wired Ribbon #11100-828 and #11194-140 for flowers; remove bottom wire; make 2, one from each ribbon
	Large Flower Centers – Beads	93	7 beads for each flower Mill Hill Antique Glass Beads #03046

"I cannot count my day complete til needle, thread and fabric meet."
~Author Unknown~

the letter E

One of my favorite embroidery stitches is the Fishbone Stitch. Look at how exquisitely Gena used her flosses and the Fishbone Stitch to grace this wreath.

Tiny Fishbone Stitch leaves add a touch of charm to flowers and bouquets in the appliqué. Notice how Lynn made the tiniest of leaves with this delicate stitch in the Stitch Sampler on page 90. Beautiful!

"E" by Gena Holland, Anderson, SC

Tip

Turning a long narrow fabric strip for a Spider Web Rose can be tricky and often frustrating. The Skinny Mini Tube Turner by Mary Kay Perry Designs is perfect for turning narrow fabric tubes for dimensional appliqué.

	Stitch/Technique	page #	Fabric/Thread/Ribbon
1	Letter E – Appliqué	10-23	12" square of background fabric 6" square of fabric for letter
2	Wreath Stem – Appliqué	24	7" square of fabric
3	Leaves – Fishbone Stitch	98	3 strands of 6-stranded cotton floss Gentle Art #7080 Endive Gentle Art #0130 Avocado Gentle Art #7082 Piney Woods Gentle Art #0112 Grasshopper
4	Small Flowers – Traveler's Joy	114	One 2¼" circle of fabric for each of the bottom petals One 1½" circle of fabric for each of the top petals
	Small Flower Centers – Colonial Knot	97	3 strands of 6-stranded cotton floss Gentle Art #7020 Butternut Squash
5	Large Flowers – Spider Web Rose	110	One 1" x width of fabric strip for each flower

"All my scattering moments are taken up with my needle."
~Ellen Birdseye Wheaton, 1851~

the letter F

Round Ruched Roses...the first time I tried "ruching in the round", I puzzled over what to do with the excess fabric and puffy center after I ruched the outside edges of the circle.

Gently pushing the center down and giving myself the freedom to allow the folds to fall where they may has worked great (along with a heavy book placed on top). Once the center is gently pressed it is ready for delicate embellishment or it is perfectly lovely as pressed.

"F" by Jo Ann Cridge, Pittsburgh, PA

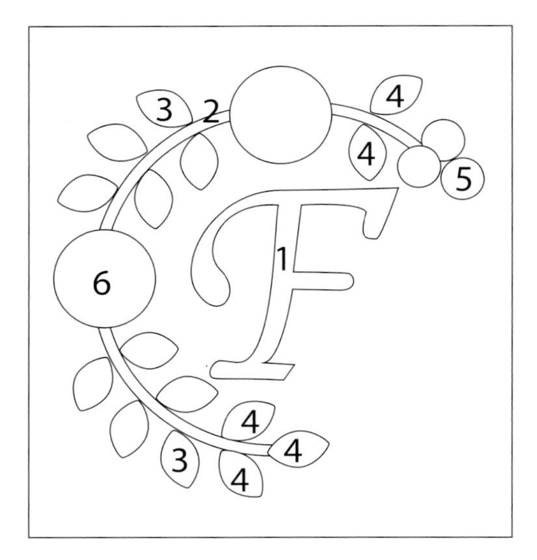

	Stitch/Technique	page #	Fabric/Thread/Ribbon
1	Letter F – Appliqué	10-23	12" square of background fabric 6" square of fabric for letter
2	Wreath Stem – Appliqué	24	7" square of fabric
3	10 Middle Leaves – Appliqué	25	Ten 2" squares of fabric
4	5 Leaves at Tips of Wreath – Fishbone Stitch	98	Superior 4 mm Silk Ribbon #SRV-04-116 Sage
5	Small Flowers – Gathered Flowers	99	Three ½" x 4½" pieces of French Ribbon Variation #0035-7
	Small Flower Centers – Beads	93	3 beads for each flower Mill Hill Glass Seed Beads #02002
6	Large Flowers – Large Round Ruched Rose	108	Two 5" squares of fabric
	Flower Center – Pistil Stitch	105	2 strands of 6-stranded cotton floss Gentle Art #7020 Butternut Squash

Tip

If you are always on the search for new tools to make your stitching easier, look to Anita Shackelford of Thimble Works for ruching tools. She has a circular ruching guide that allows you to make round ruched roses from ⅝" to 3".

"Embroidery has continually played an integral part in the history of man and woman. It not only signified certain status and wealth through the ages, but it has also given countless hours of satisfaction to those who would create something of beauty with a needle and a thread."
~Margaret Pierce~

the letter G

This is one of the few blocks where berries were used instead of small flowers on the tips of the wreath. Gena's stitch and thread selection for the berries add interest and charm to this block.

The berries were made by covering a fabric circle with Colonial Knots. The circle was then gathered and stuffed, and appliquéd to the block. The six berries coupled with the fabric Spider Web Roses make this a memorable block.

"G" by Gena Holland, Anderson, SC

Tip

Crinoline is a great product to use to make dimensional flowers off block. The Spider Web Rose is a perfect example. The flower's foundation spokes are more solid when stitched on the crinoline. It also alleviates pulling and stressing your background fabric.

	Stitch/Technique	page #	Fabric/Thread/Ribbon
1	Letter G – Appliqué	10-23	12" square of background fabric 6" square of fabric for letter
2	Wreath Stem – Appliqué	24	7" square of fabric
3	Leaves – Appliqué	25	Fifteen 2" squares of fabric
	Appliquéd Leaf Veins – Stem Stitch	112	1 strand of 6-stranded cotton floss Gentle Art #7041 Apple Cider
4	Berries – Colonial Knot Tip	97	3 strands of 6-stranded cotton floss Gentle Art #1120 Cherry Bark Gentle Art #7014 Antique Rose Gentle Art #0320 Old Brick Gentle Art #7019 Pomegranate Gentle Art #0112 Grasshopper
5	Flowers – Spider Web Rose	110	One 1" x width of fabric strip for each flower

"Take your needle, my child, and work at your pattern;
it will come out a rose by and by.
Life is like that - one stitch at a time taken patiently
and the pattern will come out all right like embroidery."
~Oliver Wendell Holmes~

the letter H

Each of the blocks in this section was made for the Alphabet Sampler quilt on page 118. The challenge of developing unique ways to use the book's eighteen stitches and techniques throughout the quilt was a creative experience for each stitcher.

On this wreath, the small Round Ruched Rose was used at the tip of the wreath. The miniature fabric roses gracefully complement the larger ribboned ruched roses.

"H" by Janice Vaine, Jacksonville, FL

	Stitch/Technique	page #	Fabric/Thread/Ribbon
1	Letter H – Appliqué	10-23	12" square of background fabric 6" square of fabric for letter
2	Wreath Stem – Raised Stem Stitch	106	3 strands of 6-stranded cotton floss Gentle Art #7082 Piney Woods
3	Leaves – Appliqué	25	Fifteen 2" squares of fabric
4	Small Flowers – Small Round Ruched Rose	108	Six 3" squares of fabric
	Small Flower Centers – Colonial Knot	97	3 strands of 6-stranded cotton floss Gentle Art #0320 Old Brick Gentle Art #0112 Grasshopper
5	Large Flowers – Jan's Ruched Rose	100	One ⅝" x 33" piece of French Ombré Wired Ribbon #00471-63 for each flower; remove wire from bottom; make 2
	Large Flower Centers – Colonial Knot	97	3 strands of 6-stranded cotton floss Gentle Art #0320 Old Brick

Tip

Here's a tip from Gena Holland. When forming a ruched rose, secure the five-petaled center to a piece of crinoline. Wrap the ruched strip around the center, securing it to the crinoline to form the rose.

Gena finds this helps maintain a round rose rather than an oblong or egg-shaped flower.

"O Lord Thy grace divine impart, And let my Bible be
A guardian angel to my heart, To lead my soul to Thee."
~On an embroidery sampler by Mary Everett, 11 years old, dated December 20, 1806~

the letter I

The simplicity of this block makes it elegant. The Gathered Flowers made with beautiful French Ombré ribbon and flower centers filled with silk ribbon Colonial Knots nestled among the clean lines of the appliquéd stem and leaves come together in understated sophistication.

"I" by Gena Holland, Anderson, SC

	Stitch/Technique	page #	Fabric/Thread/Ribbon
1	Letter I – Appliqué	10-23	12" square of background fabric 6" square of fabric for letter
2	Wreath Stem – Appliqué	24	7" square of fabric
3	Leaves – Appliqué	25	Twenty 2" squares of fabric
	Appliquéd Leaf Veins – Stem Stitch	112	1 strand of 6-stranded cotton floss Gentle Art #7041 Apple Cider
4	Flowers – Gathered Flowers	99	One ⅝" x 24" piece of French Ombré Wired Ribbon #49-1 for each flower; make 4
	Flower Centers – Colonial Knot	97	Superior 4mm Silk Ribbon #SRV-04-107 Daffodil

Tip

When gathering the ribbon for the Gathered Flower, allow the ribbon to wrap around itself, making multiple layers with one gathered circle behind the other.

Experiment with different lengths of ribbon and gathering the thread looser or tighter to achieve varying results.

"As I work among my flowers, I find myself talking to them, reasoning and remonstrating with them and adoring them as if they were human beings.
Much laughter I provoke among my friends by so doing, but that is of no consequence.
We are on such good terms, my flowers and I."
~Celia Thaxter, 1835-1894~

the letter J

This block uses multiple small Bachelor Buttons grouped together to form two larger flower balls. The variation of color from the batik fabric gives a realism to the flowers, almost as though the sunlight is dancing over the light and dark shades of the petals.

Ribbon embroidery leaves intermingle with the appliquéd leaves to add even more dimension.

"J" by Sonnie Cridge, Pittsburgh, PA

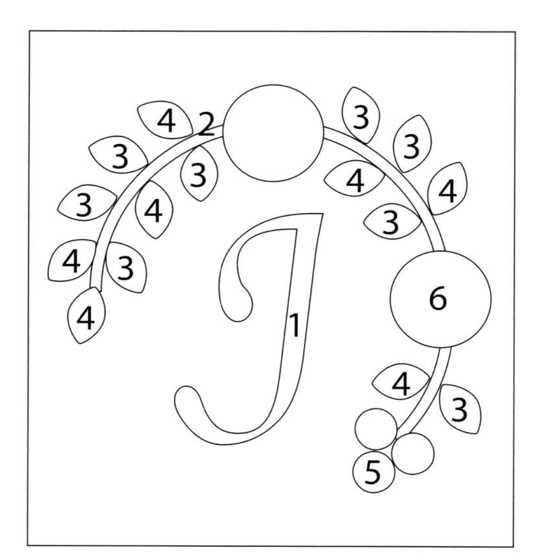

	Stitch/Technique	page #	Fabric/Thread/Ribbon
1	Letter J – Appliqué	10-23	12" square of background fabric 6" square of fabric for letter
2	Wreath Stem – Appliqué	24	7" square of fabric
3	8 Leaves – Appliqué	25	Eight 2" squares of fabric
4	7 Leaves – Fishbone Stitch	98	Superior 2mm Silk Ribbon #SRV-02-129 Serengeti Superior 4mm Silk Ribbon #SRV-04-114 Eucalyptus #SRV-04-116 Sage #SRV-04-131 Vine
5	Small Flowers – Bachelor Buttons	92	One 1½" circle of fabric for each of the bottom petals One 1" circle of fabric for each of the top petals
	Flower Centers – Colonial Knot	97	3 strands of 6-stranded cotton floss Gentle Art #7020 Butternut Squash
6	Large Flowers – Bachelor Buttons	92	One 1½" circle of fabric for each of the bottom petals One 1" circle of fabric for each of the top petals
	Flower Centers – Colonial Knot	97	3 strands of 6-stranded cotton floss Gentle Art #7020 Butternut Squash

Tip

When using a varigated thread or ribbon on a project make a sample of the stitch first. This will help you determine if the variegation is a soft transition or too hard lined for the chosen technique.

Stitching a sample before adding the stitch and thread to the block lessens the stress levels.

"Creativity is allowing yourself to make mistakes. Art is knowing which ones to keep."
-Scott Adams-
'The Dilbert Principle', US cartoonist (1957 -)

the letter K

The K is the first letter stitched in two pieces. This ensures a sharp point in the middle of the K.

The wreath is made with fabric Boat Leaves from the same piece of batik fabric. They are a lovely complement to the Raised Stem Stitch wreath stem. Add the Gathered Flower made with French Ombré Wired Ribbon and you have a block that will gain rave reviews.

"K" by Gena Holland, Anderson, SC

Tip

When faced with a narrow stem, a new appliquér may be a bit intimidated. Although the Perfect Placement Method will work narrow stems smoothly and with ease, embroidery can be substituted for the appliqué.

The Raised Stem Stitch worked with cotton floss or Simply Wool, or the Ribbon Stitch worked with 2mm of silk ribbon (see page 80) are beautiful substitutions for appliquéd stems.

	Stitch/Technique	page #	Fabric/Thread/Ribbon
1	Letter K – Appliqué	10-23	12" square of background fabric 6" square of fabric for letter
2	Wreath Stem – Raised Stem Stitch	106	2 strands of 6-stranded cotton floss Gentle Art #7041 Apple Cider
3	Leaves – Boat Leaf	94	Sixteen 1" x 3¾" pieces of fabric
4	Flower – Gathered Flowers	99	One ⅝" x 30" piece of French Ombré Wired Ribbon #00471-63
	Flower Center – Colonial Knot	97	Superior 4mm Silk Ribbon #SRV-04-107 Daffodil

"Life is like a rose...More exquisite and precious,
When shared with others."
~Jane Oechsle Lauer~

the letter L

Half wreath blocks are my favorite. It is a perfect block for beginners, as well as a creative challenge for experienced stitchers. Add a letter of your choice, the leaf technique you prefer, and one of the many flowers in the book for the center of the wreath.

This block lends itself to artistic interpretation and many variations. This Petal Flower was made with two rows of petals. Make one flower on a 2" circle and one flower on a 1½" circle. Offset the petals of the two flowers, join together and add a center.

"L" by Janice Vaine, Jacksonville, FL

Tip

After you have mastered the 18 stitches and techniques found within these pages, take your stitching journey to the next level, experimenting with additional stitches and techniques found in "The Art of Elegant Hand Embroidery, Embellishment and Appliqué" by Janice Vaine.

	Stitch/Technique	page #	Fabric/Thread/Ribbon
1	Letter L – Appliqué	10-23	12" square of background fabric 6" square of fabric for letter
2	Wreath Stem – Appliqué	24	7" square of fabric
3	10 Bottom Leaves – Appliqué	25	Ten 2" squares of fabric for leaves on left and right of center flower
	Appliquéd Leaf Veins – Stem Stitch and Straight Stitch	112 113	1 strand of 6-stranded cotton floss Gentle Art #0130 Avocado
4	6 Top Leaves – Fishbone Stitch	98	Superior 4mm silk ribbon #SRV-04-116 Sage
5	Flower – Petal Flower	104	Eight 2¾" circles of fabric. Make one 8-petal flower on a 2" circle and one 8-petal flower on a 1½" circle. Offset the two flowers and join together.
	Center – Small Round Ruched Rose and Beads	108 93	One 3" square of fabric 7 Mill Hill Glass Seed Beads #00968

"So you see, imagination needs noodling - long, inefficient, happy idling, dawdling and puttering."
~Brenda Ueland~

the letter M

During your appliqué journey, you will discover there are few appliqué patterns that do not incorporate leaves in one shape or another. Each block in this book affords you the opportunity to practice perfecting your leaves.

One tip for appliquéing sharp points on leaves is redrawing or reshaping the leaf point in order to appliqué a crisp, sharp corner.

Nature gives us leaves in all shapes and sizes. Make each leaf your own.

"M" by Gena Holland, Anderson, SC

Tip

Gathered Flowers make a stunning carnation. Make two Gathered Flowers from two 18" lengths of ribbon. Make two flowers, gathering one more tightly than the other. Place the flower with the tighter gathers on top of the loosely gathered flower and stitch together, hiding the stitches in the folds of the petals.

	Stitch/Technique	page #	Fabric/Thread/Ribbon
1	Letter M – Appliqué	10-23	12" square of background fabric 6" square of fabric for letter
2	Wreath Stem – Appliqué	24	7" square of fabric
3	Leaves – Appliqué	25	Fifteen 2" squares of fabric
4	Small Flowers – Bachelor Buttons	92	One 1½" circle of fabric for each of the bottom petals One 1" circle of fabric for each of the top petals
	Small Flower Centers – Colonial Knot	97	2 strands of 6-stranded cotton floss Gentle Art #7020 Butternut Squash
5	Large Flowers – Gathered Flowers	99	One ⅝" x 30" piece of French Ombré Wired Ribbon #00471-63 for each flower
	Large Flower Centers – Traveler's Joy and Colonial Knot	114 97	One 1" circle of fabric for each flower 2 strands of 6-stranded cotton floss Gentle Art #7020 Butternut Squash

"One of the advantages of being disorderly is that one is constantly making exciting discoveries."
~A. A. Milne~
English children's author (1882 - 1956)

the letter N

I love how this block combines appliquéd leaves with embroidered Fishbone Stitch leaves. The variation of colors within the appliquéd batik leaves allowed for the use of several colors of embroidery flosses in the Fishbone Stitch leaves.

The appliqué and embroidery techniques blend beautifully around the wreath.

"N" by Jo Ann Cridge, Pittsburgh, PA

Tip

Did you notice all the flowers on this block are Spider Web Roses? The smaller roses were worked with embroidery floss and the larger roses with a luscious hand-dyed silk ribbon.

Experiment with different threads or ribbons when trying a new stitch or technique.

	Stitch/Technique	page #	Fabric/Thread/Ribbon
1	Letter N – Appliqué	10-23	12" square of background fabric 6" square of fabric for letter
2	Wreath Stem – Appliqué	24	7" square of fabric
3	Leaves – Appliqué	25	Ten 2" squares of fabric
4	Leaves – Fishbone Stitch	98	3 strands of 6-stranded cotton floss Gentle Art #0130 Avocado Gentle Art #0110 Dried Thyme Gentle Art #0190 Forest Glade
5	Small Flowers – Spider Web Rose	110	3 strands of 6-stranded cotton floss Gentle Art #7008 Rhubarb
	Small Flower Centers – Colonial Knot	97	3 strands of 6-stranded cotton floss Gentle Art #1120 Cherry Bark
6	Large Flowers – Spider Web Rose	110	Superior 7mm Silk Ribbon #SRV-07-127 A Dozen Roses

"If I have ever made any valuable discoveries,
it has been owing more to patient attention, than to any other talent."
~Isaac Newton~
English mathematician & physicist (1642 - 1727)

the letter O

This block illustrates ribbonwork at its finest with silk ribbon Spider Web Roses and Boat Leaves made with wired French Ombré ribbon.

The dainty Traveler's Joy flowers at the tip of the wreath add just the right touch of dimension to complete the block. Notice how the darker back petals of the Traveler's Joy make the tiny top petals appear to be sitting in a calyx.

"O" by Gena Holland, Anderson, SC

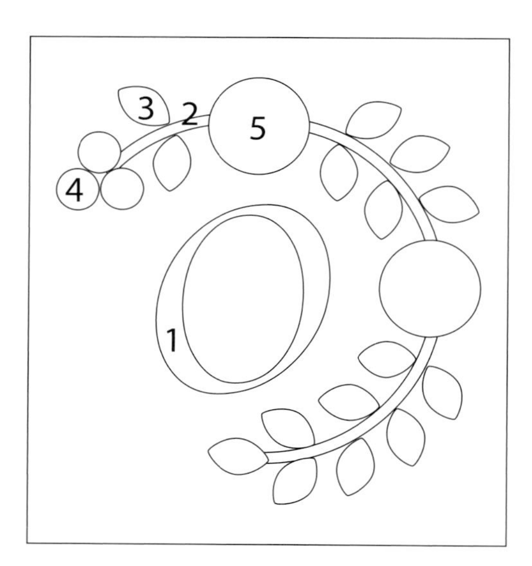

Tip

Spider Web Roses work up beautifully in ribbon or fabric. When weaving the rose, allow the ribbon or fabric to naturally twist as you go over and under the foundation spokes.

	Stitch/Technique	page #	Fabric/Thread/Ribbon
1	Letter O – Appliqué	10-23	12" square of background fabric 6" square of fabric for letter
2	Wreath Stem – Appliqué	24	7" square of fabric
3	Leaves – Boat Leaf	94	Five each ⅝" x 3½" pieces of French Ombré Wired Ribbon #48-9, #49-7, and #49-12
4	Small Flowers – Traveler's Joy	114	One 2" circle of fabric for each of the bottom petals One 1½" circle of fabric for each of the top petals
	Small Flower Centers – Colonial Knot	97	3 strands of 6-stranded cotton floss Gentle Art #7020 Butternut Squash
5	Large Flowers – Spider Web Rose	110	Superior 7mm Silk Ribbon #SRV-07-103 Hyacinth

"To accomplish great things, we must dream as well as act."
~Anatole France~
French novelist (1844 - 1924)

the letter P

The P block illustrates another use for the Stem Stitch, one of the most basic embroidery stitches. Take a close look at the berries. They were filled with rounds of Stem Stitches, working from the outside into the center.

The Stem Stitch is useful for outlining and stitching details within a design and is also a good filling stitch.

"P" by Luella Dusek, Pittsburgh, PA

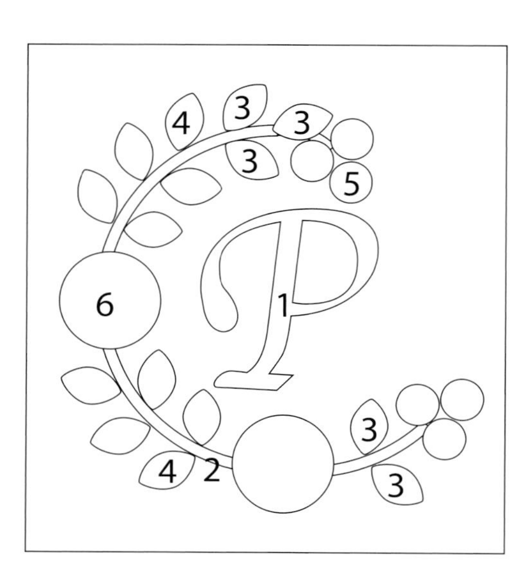

Tip

Fishbone Stitch leaves may also be worked with the threads consistently spaced farther apart between stitches. This gives the leaf a lacy, airy effect.

	Stitch/Technique	page #	Fabric/Thread/Ribbon
1	Letter P – Appliqué	10-23	12" square of background fabric 6" square of fabric for letter
2	Wreath Stem – Appliqué	24	7" square of fabric
3	Leaves – Appliqué	25	Five 2" squares of fabric
4	Leaves – Fishbone Stitch	98	3 strands of 6-stranded cotton floss Gentle Art #7080 Endive
5	Small Flowers – Stem Stitch	112	3 strands of 6-stranded cotton floss Gentle Art #7019 Pomegranate
6	Large Flowers – Bachelor Buttons	92	Cut the following five circles of fabric for each flower: 4", 3¾", 3", 2¼", 1½" Make 2 flowers
	Large Flower Centers – Beads	93	3 beads for each flower

“The wisest mind has something yet to learn.”
~ George Santayana ~
US (Spanish-born) philosopher (1863 - 1952)

the letter Q

The Q block showcases fabric Gathered Flowers, which are a delightful surprise depending on the print of the fabric. Can you envision the abundance of flowers in the garden when the Gathered Flower is made with fabric?

Notice the tiny Traveler's Joys with Colonial Knots in the center of the Gathered Flowers. Simply precious.

"Q" by Gena Holland, Anderson, SC

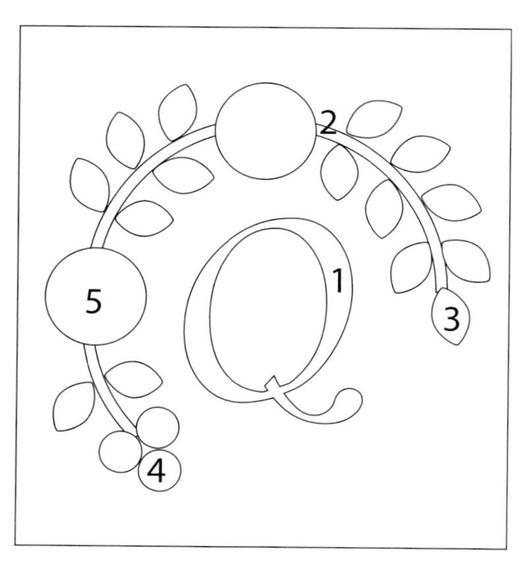

Tip

The Traveler's Joy stitching instructions call for two circles to form the top and lower petals of the flower. Make a third flower with a 2½" circle of green fabric. Offset it on the bottom of the two-layered flower when stitching to form a calyx on the tiny flowers.

	Stitch/Technique	page #	Fabric/Thread/Ribbon
1	Letter Q – Appliqué	10-23	12" square of background fabric 6" square of fabric for letter
2	Wreath Stem – Appliqué	24	7" square of fabric
3	Leaves – Appliqué	25	Fifteen 2" squares of fabric
4	Small Flowers – Traveler's Joy	114	One 2" circle of fabric for each of the bottom petals One 1½" circle of fabric for each of the middle petals One 1" circle of fabric for each of the top petals
	Small Flower Centers – Colonial Knot	97	2 strands of 6-stranded cotton floss Gentle Art #7020 Butternut Squash
5	Large Flowers – Gathered Flowers	99	One 2" x 14" strip of fabric for each flower
	Flower Centers – Traveler's Joy and Colonial Knot	114 97	One 1" circle of fabric for each flower center 2 strands of 6-stranded cotton floss Gentle Art #7020 Butternut Squash

"Have patience with all things, but chiefly have patience with yourself. Do not lose courage in considering your own imperfections but instantly set about remedying them - every day begin the task anew."

~Saint Francis de Sales~

French saint & bishop of Geneva (1567 - 1622)

the letter R

The R block showcases Jan's Ruched Rose highlighted by embroidered Fishbone Stitch leaves.

Use French Ombré wired ribbon to make the five-petal center of the rose. Wrap the second round of petals behind the rose center. Then flip the ribbon and complete the flower. This technique, coupled with the French Ombré ribbon, gives the flower a light interior and darker outer edges.

The flower centers will twinkle with the addition of several glass beads.

"R" by Janice Vaine, Jacksonville, FL

Tip

When using a 1" wide ribbon to make Jan's Ruched Rose, fold the top edge down 3⁄16" and press for the five ½" petals and the eight ¾" petals. Use the full ribbon width to make the remaining eighteen 1¼" petals.

	Stitch/Technique	page #	Fabric/Thread/Ribbon
1	Letter R – Appliqué	10-23	12" square of background fabric 6" square of fabric for letter
2	Wreath Stem – Appliqué	24	8" square of fabric
3	Leaves – Fishbone Stitch	98	3 strands of 6-stranded cotton floss Gentle Art #0110 Dried Thyme Gentle Art #0112 Grasshopper Gentle Art #0130 Avocado Gentle Art #0190 Forest Glade Gentle Art #7080 Endive
4	Flowers – Jan's Ruched Rose	100	One 1" x 33" piece of French Ombré Wired Ribbon #48-3 for each flower; remove wire from bottom edge; make 4
	Flower Centers – Beads	93	5-6 beads for each flower Mill Hill Glass Beads #02077

"Have courage for the great sorrows of life and patience for the small ones; and when you have laboriously accomplished your daily task, go to sleep in peace. God is awake."

~Victor Hugo~

French dramatist, novelist, & poet (1802 - 1885)

the letter S

After making and applying the Round Ruched Roses to this block, Gena added a spark of interest with glorious Ribbon Stitch petals and Colonial Knots made with softly variegated silk ribbons.

A simple and inspiring use of techniques and fibers.

"S" by Gena Holland, Anderson, SC

	Stitch/Technique	page #	Fabric/Thread/Ribbon
1	Letter S – Appliqué	10-23	12" square of background fabric 6" square of fabric for letter
2	Wreath Stem – Appliqué	24	8" square of fabric
3	Leaves – Appliqué	25	Twenty 2" squares of fabric
4	Flowers – Large Round Ruched Rose	108	Four 5" squares of fabric
	Flower Centers – Ribbon Stitch	107	Superior 7mm Silk Ribbon #SRV-07-127 A Dozen Roses
	Ribbon Stitch Flower Centers – Colonial Knot	97	Superior 4mm Silk Ribbon #SRV-04-116 Sage

Tip

When attaching dimensional flowers and embellishments to an appliqué design, place the block in an embroidery hoop for ease in stitching. Be sure the hoop encompasses the whole design so as not to distort or crush the appliqué or other embellishments.

"By perseverance the snail reached the ark."
~Charles Haddon Spurgeon~
English preacher (1834 - 1892)

the letter T

The T block is a simple lesson in beading. One small single bead in the center of each Gathered Ribbon Flower and one at the tips of the small Straight Stitch flowers add a touch of sparkle to this block.

Beading is an easy way to add interest to a block, project, or quilt. Try substituting beads for Colonial Knots to highlight a flower center.

"T" by Janice Vaine, Jacksonville, FL

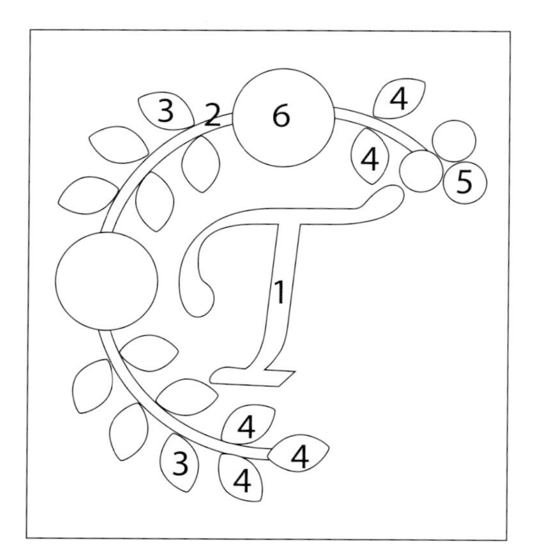

Tip

If using the Pistil Stitch for the small flowers at the top of the wreath, appliqué the end of the wreath stem. The airiness of this little flower will not cover raw edges at the end of the stem.

	Stitch/Technique	page #	Fabric/Thread/Ribbon
1	Letter T – Appliqué	10-23	12" square of background fabric 6" square of fabric for letter
2	Wreath Stem – Appliqué	24	7" square of fabric
3	Leaves – Appliqué	25	Ten 2" squares of fabric for leaves on the left side of the wreath
4	Leaves – Boat Leaf	94	One 1" x 3¾" strip of fabric for each leaf; make 5
5	Small Flowers – Straight Stitch and Beads	113 93	3 strands of 6-stranded cotton floss Gentle Art #1120 Cherry Bark Mill Hill Glass Seed Beads #02076
6	Large Flowers – Gathered Flowers	99	One ½" x 4½" piece of French Ribbon Variation #0035-10 for each flower; make 7 flowers for each cluster
	Large Flower Centers – Beads	93	1 bead for each flower center Mill Hill Glass Seed Beads #02080

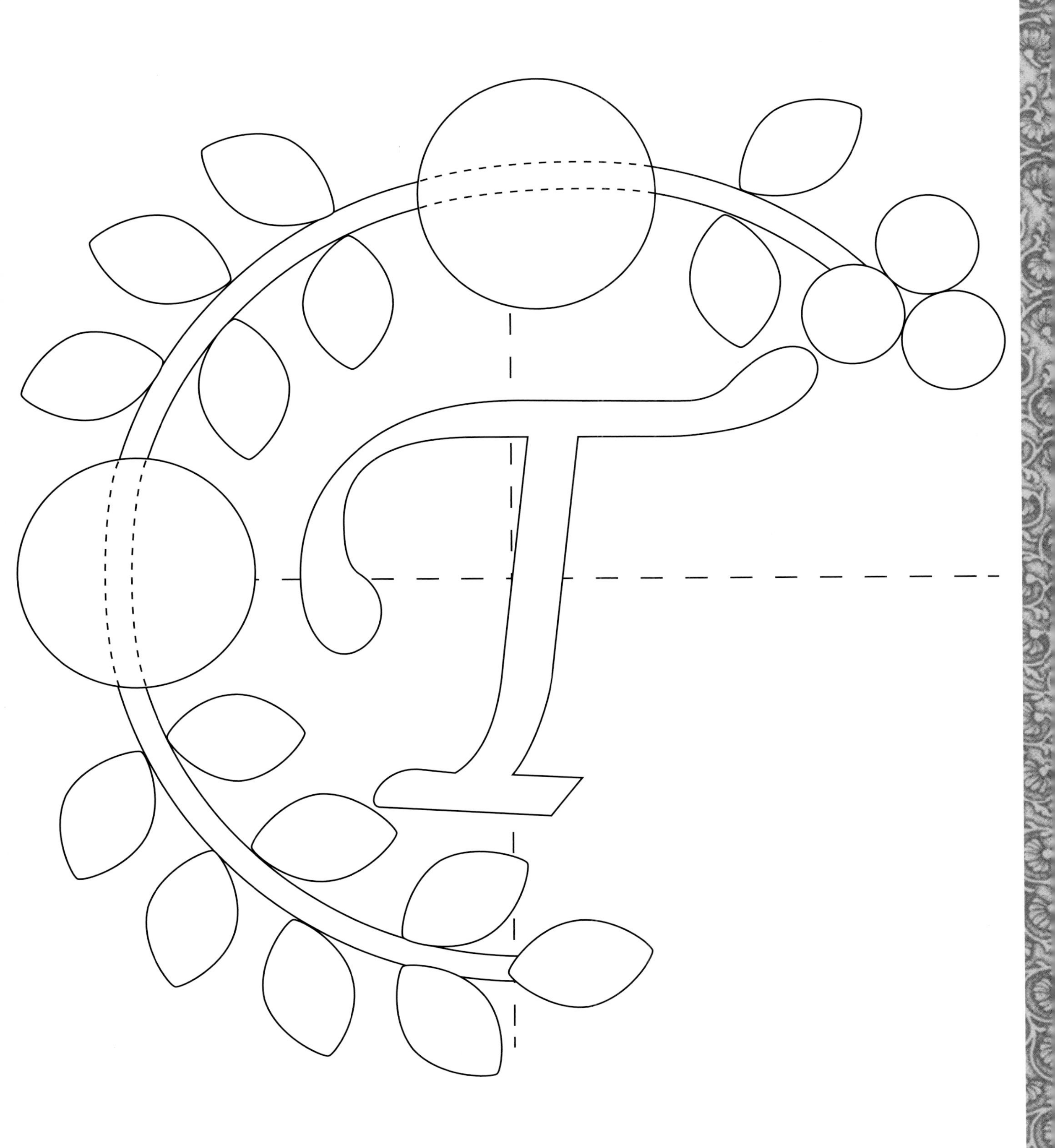

"That which we persist in doing becomes easier, not that the task itself has become easier, but that our ability to perform it has improved."
~Ralph Waldo Emerson~
US essayist & poet (1803 - 1882)

the letter U

The Bullion Knot is a unique little stitch. It is most widely known for its use in making bullion roses and flower calyxes.

The Bullion Knot also makes petite petalled flowers. In this block they highlight the small Traveler's Joy in the center of the Gathered Flowers.

For additional inspiration, look at the Bullion Knot calyxes surrounding the ribboned rose buds on the Stitch Sampler on page 90. Lovely!

"U" by Gena Holland, Anderson, SC

Tip

Use a cotton-covered polyester thread for gathering fabric or silk. A slick thread, such as silk, will not hold the gathers.

Tug on the thread while it is still on the spool to check for breakage. Thread does have a lifespan. If it breaks coming off the spool it will break while gathering.

	Stitch/Technique	page #	Fabric/Thread/Ribbon
1	Letter U – Appliqué	10-23	12" square of background fabric 6" square of fabric for letter
2	Wreath Stem – Appliqué	24	7" square of fabric
3	Leaves – Appliqué	25	Fifteen 2" squares of fabric
	Leaf Veins – Stem Stitch	112	1 strand of 6-stranded cotton floss Gentle Art #7082 Piney Woods
4	Small Flowers – Traveler's Joy	114	One 2" circle of fabric for each of the bottom petals One 1½" circle of fabric for each of the top petals
	Small Flower Centers – Colonial Knot	97	2 strands of 6-stranded cotton floss Gentle Art #7020 Butternut Squash
5	Large Flowers – Gathered Flowers	99	One 2" x 8" strip of fabric for each flower
	Large Flower Centers – Bullion Knot around Traveler's Joy filled with Colonial Knot	96 114 97	Each Bullion Knot: 20 wraps of 3 strands of 6-stranded cotton floss Gentle Art #7023 Green Pasture Traveler's Joy: One 1" circle of fabric for each flower Colonial Knot: 2 strands of 6-stranded cotton floss Gentle Art #7020 Butternut Squash

"Just because something doesn't do what you planned it to do doesn't mean it's useless."
~ Thomas A. Edison ~
US inventor (1847 - 1931)

the letter V

There are several techniques to take note of on this block. Jan's Ruched Roses were made with fabric, which gives surprising results when it is gathered and ruched.

The wreath stem application was stitched using the Raised Stem Stitch and silk ribbon to create a lovely detail.

"V" by Janice Vaine, Jacksonville, FL

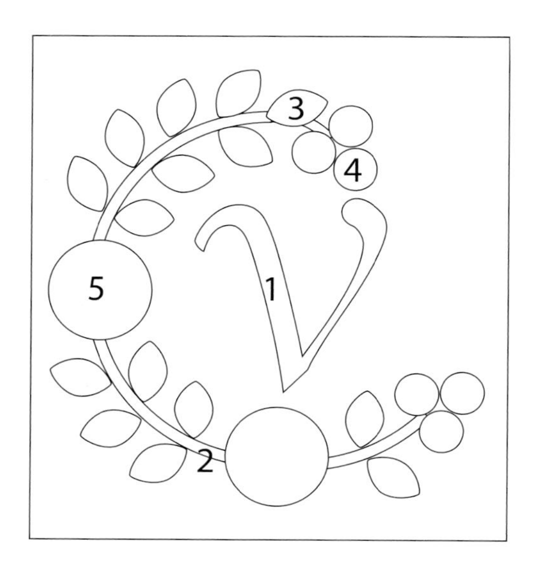

Tip

When padding appliqué, try wool batting. It adds a nice dimension to padded appliqué.

Choose a small busy print for appliquéd circles. Your circles will appear rounder and closer to perfection.

	Stitch/Technique	page #	Fabric/Thread/Ribbon
1	Letter V – Appliqué	10-23	12" square of background fabric 6" square of fabric for letter
2	Wreath Stem – Raised Stem Stitch	106	Foundation Stitches ¼" apart – Gentle Art Simply Wool #0440-W Maple Syrup Raised Stem Stitches – Superior 2mm silk ribbon #SRV-02-129 Serengeti
3	Leaves – Appliqué	25	Fifteen 2" squares of fabric
4	Berries – Padded Circles	24	Six 2" squares of fabric Twelve 1½" squares of batting for padding
5	Large Flowers – Jan's Ruched Rose	100	One 1¼" x 33" strip of fabric for each flower; make 2
	Large Flower Centers – Beads	93	3 beads for each flower center

"Take rest; a field that has rested gives a bountiful crop."
-Ovid-
Roman poet (43 BC - 17 AD)

the letter W

Hand-dyed, variegated silk ribbon is used for stitching the Fishbone Stitch leaves in this block. The hand-dyed ribbon adds subtle or defined color changes to the embroidered leaves. Both are equally beautiful.

The center of the Spider Web Rose is made by covering a fabric circle with Colonial Knots. This is the same method used for the berries on the G block on page 50. Same technique, different application, exquisite results for both.

"W" by Gena Holland, Anderson, SC

	Stitch/Technique	page #	Fabric/Thread/Ribbon
1	Letter W – Appliqué	10-23	12" square of background fabric 6" square of fabric for letter
2	Wreath Stem – Appliqué	24	7" square of fabric
3	Leaves – Fishbone Stitch	98	Superior 4mm Silk Ribbon #SRV-04-114 Eucalyptus #SRV-04-116 Sage #SRV-04-131 Vine
4	Flower – Spider Web Rose	110	One 1" x width of fabric strip
	Flower Center – Colonial Knot Tip	97	3 strands of 6-stranded cotton floss Gentle Art #1120 Cherry Bark

Tip

When working with silk ribbon, press the ribbon using the silk setting on the iron before stitching or forming flowers. Gently pull the ribbon under the iron with one hand while holding the iron with the other.

"Teachers open the door. You enter by yourself."
~Chinese Proverb~

the letter X

This block is full of wonderful embellishing possibilites.

The Petal Flowers are embellished with a small Round Ruched Rose and silk ribbon Colonial Knots. The Boat Leaves encircling the wreath were made with a batik fabric giving the look of nature's own variegation. The precious little flowers at wreath's end are circles of Ribbon Stitches made with softly variegated silk ribbon.

All these techniques blend together adding beautiful dimension to a simple block.

"X" by Luella Dusek, Pittsburgh, PA

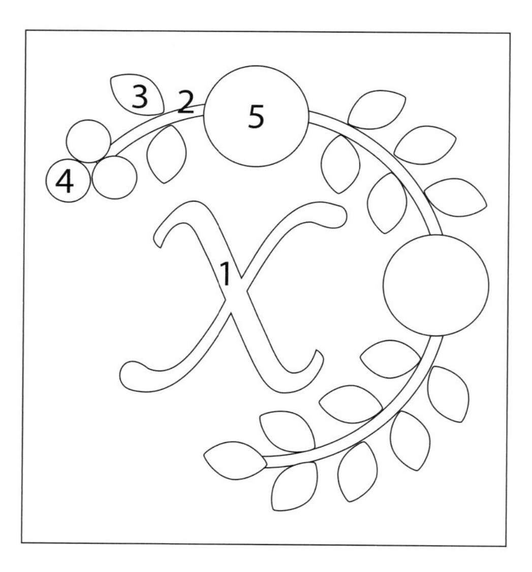

	Stitch/Technique	page #	Fabric/Thread/Ribbon
1	Letter X – Appliqué	10-23	12" square of background fabric 6" square of fabric for letter
2	Wreath Stem – Appliqué	24	7" square of fabric
3	Leaves – Boat Leaf	94	Fifteen 1" x 3¾" pieces of fabric
4	Small Flowers – Ribbon Stitch	107	Superior 4mm Silk Ribbon #SRV-04-120 Bachelor Buttons
	Small Flower Centers – Colonial Knot	97	Superior 4mm Silk Ribbon #SRV-04-107 Daffodil
5	Large Flowers – Petal Flower	104	Four 2¼" circles for each flower
	Large Flower Centers – Small Round Ruched Rose and Colonial Knot	108 97	Two 3" squares of fabric for each small flower Superior 4mm Silk Ribbon #SRV-04-107 Daffodil

Tip

The Ribbon Stitch may also be used to make a stem by laying the stitches diagonally side by side. A variegated ribbon provides a lovely wreath stem on any one of the blocks.

"The great French Marshall Lyautey once asked his gardener to plant a tree.
The gardener objected that the tree was slow growing and would not reach maturity for 100 years.
The Marshall replied, 'In that case, there is no time to lose; plant it this afternoon!'"
-John F. Kennedy-
35th president of US 1961-1963 (1917 - 1963)

the letter Y

This block illustrates how appliqué can be enhanced with simple touches of embroidered embellishment.

The appliquéd leaves gain an extra layer of dimension with the addition of the Stem Stitched veins. The Pistil Stitches dance in the center of the Round Ruched Roses and three little Colonial Knots in the middle of the Bachelor Buttons give the flowers a finishing touch.

"Y" by Gena Holland, Anderson, SC

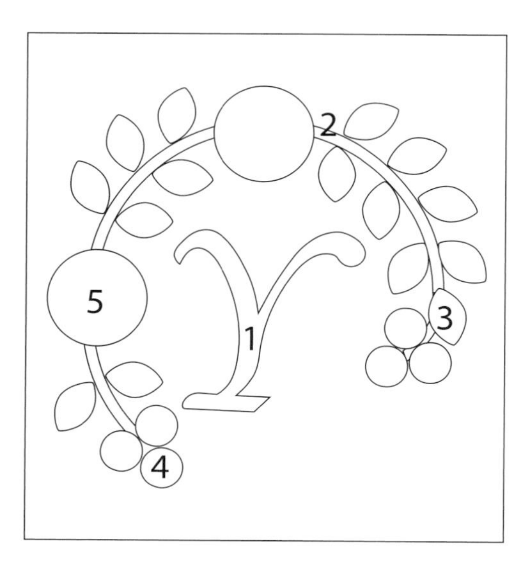

Tip

If you are now hooked on the Perfect Placement Appliqué method, try placing the block on a sandpaper board to hold it in place while you are tracing around the outer edges of the basting stitches. This will give you smoother lines.

	Stitch/Technique	page #	Fabric/Thread/Ribbon
1	Letter Y – Appliqué	10-23	12" square of background fabric 6" square of fabric for letter
2	Wreath Stem – Appliqué	24	7" square of fabric
3	Leaves – Appliqué	25	Fifteen 2" squares of fabric
	Appliquéd Leaf Veins – Stem Stitch	112	1 strand of 6-stranded cotton floss Gentle Art #7041 Apple Cider
4	Small Flowers – Bachelor Buttons	92	One 1½" circle of fabric for each of the bottom petals One 1" circle of fabric for each of the top petals
	Small Flower Centers – Colonial Knot	97	2 strands of 6-stranded cotton floss Gentle Art #7020 Butternut Squash
5	Large Flowers – Large Round Ruched Rose	108	Two 5" squares of fabric
	Large Flower Centers – Pistil Stitch and Colonial Knot	105 97	3 strands of 6-stranded cotton floss Gentle Art #7020 Butternut Squash

"Time cools, time clarifies; no mood can be maintained quite unaltered through the course of hours."
-Mark Twain-
US humorist, novelist, short story author, & wit (1835 - 1910)

the letter Z

Traveler's Joys have been used on other blocks for the small flowers at the tips of the wreath. In the Z block, five Traveler's Joys were grouped together to form a flower blossom.

The combining of batik fabric appliquéd leaves and embroidered leaves add subtle dimension and interest to your designs.

May the suggested stitches used in the A through Z blocks inspire your creativity and encourage you to try the book's stitches in unique ways.

"Z" by Luella Dusek, Pittsburgh, PA

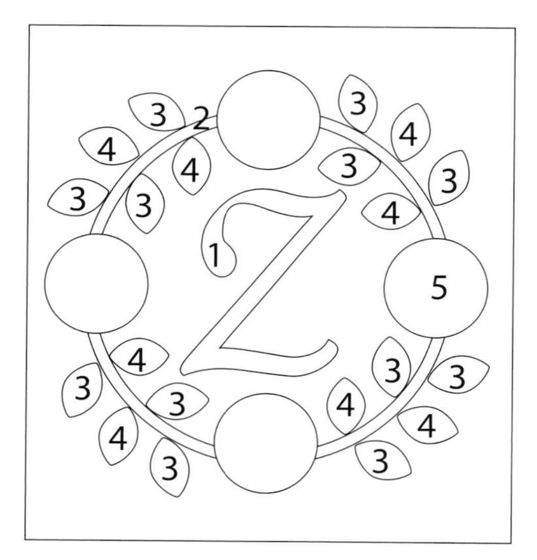

	Stitch/Technique	page #	Fabric/Thread/Ribbon
1	Letter Z – Appliqué	10-23	12" square of background fabric 6" square of fabric for letter
2	Wreath Stem – Appliqué	24	8" square of fabric
3	Leaves – Appliqué	25	Twelve 2" squares of fabric
	Appliquéd Leaf Veins – Stem Stitch and Straight Stitch	112 113	1 strand of 6-stranded cotton floss Gentle Art #0110 Dried Thyme
4	Leaves – Fishbone Stitch	98	3 strands of 6-stranded cotton floss Gentle Art #7080 Endive
5	Flowers – Traveler's Joy	114	One 2" circle of fabric for each of the bottom petals One 1¼" circle of fabric for each of the top petals
	Flower Centers – Colonial Knot	97	3 strands of 6-stranded cotton floss Gentle Art #7019 Pomegranate

Tip

Here's a tip from my Mom to help you make consistent petals on the Traveler's Joys.

When forming the flower petals, after wrapping the thread over and around the edge of the circle keep your thumb firmly on the thread while pulling the thread to gather and form the petals.

"Measure not the work until the day's out and the labor done."
-Elizabeth Barrett Browning-
English poet (1806 - 1861)

Stitch Sampler, 25" x 25"
by Lynn Rogers and Janice Vaine; quilted by Marilyn Lange

More Stitches

embroidery & embellishment

em·broi·der·y [em bróyd ree]

1. *act of making decorative needlework: the craft of using needlework to make decorative designs*
2. *something with decorative needlework: something produced by or ornamented with decorative needlework*
3. *embellishment of story: elaboration or embellishment added to make an account of something more interesting*

Encarta World English Dictionary

The term embroidery often conjures up the idea of stitches worked with embroidery floss. Yet, as the opening definition implies, this term could encompass stitches worked with ribbon, stumpwork or raised embroidery. Even the dimensional techniques such as the Petal Flowers and Round Ruched Flower found in this chapter fit the term. Embroidery is a multitude of embellishments which adds interest and dimension to needlework.

In centuries past, young ladies had a needle and thread placed in their hands at a very young age. Needlework was part of their education, often more important than learning to read and write. If you walk through the fine arts galleries of today's museums, you will see numerous samplers designed and stitched by girls as young as five, attesting to their skill, as well as needlework's place in history.

This chapter highlights several basic embroidery stitches to complement and embellish appliqué. Some of the stitches may even be familiar to you, stitches your mother, grandmother or aunt may have shown you when you were young. The beauty of these simple stitches is their adaptability and the variety they offer to enhance your appliqué.

Learn the stitches on the following pages and then combine them to embellish your own unique appliqué needlework design. Maybe one day your needlework will attest to the beauty of the needle art of our time.

Stitch Sampler

	Column 1	*Column 2*	*Column 3*	*Column 4*
Row A	*Bachelor Buttons*	*Colonial Knot*	*Traveler's Joy*	*Jan's Ruched Rose*
Row B	*Gathered Flowers*	*Large Round Ruched Rose*	*Ribbon Stitch & Colonial Knot*	*Straight Stitch & Colonial Knot*
Row C	*Pistil Stitch & Colonial Knot*	*"A" Stem Stitched*	*Spider Web Rose*	*Gathered Flowers & Beads*
Row D	*Gathered Flowers*	*Ribbon Stitch & Bullion Knot*	*Boat Leaf*	*Petal Flower & Gathered Flowers*

Note: All the stems were worked with the Stem Stitch. All the leaves are worked with the Fishbone Stitch with the exception of A2 which are made with the Ribbon Stitch and D3 which are Boat Leaves. The blocks are 4" finished.

the stitch Bachelor Buttons

This pretty little flower lends itself to creative interpretation, whether making it with various size circles or embellishing the center with embroidery, stumpwork, or ribbonwork.

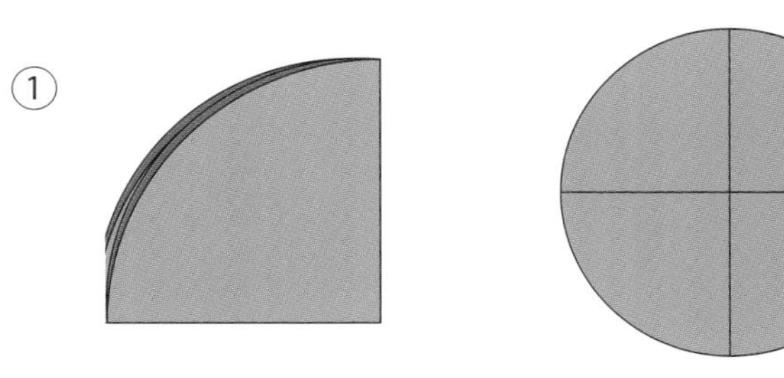

1. Cut one 2" circle and one 1½" circle. Fold each of the circles in half twice, quartering it. Fingerpress the folds.

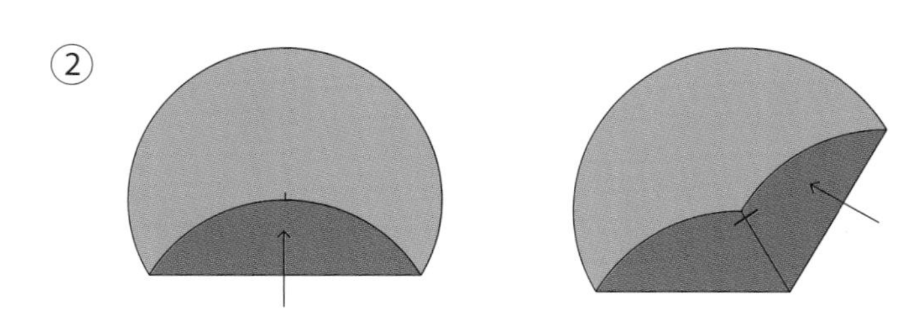

2. Beginning with the larger circle, fold the bottom edge of the circle to the center. Fold the right corner to the center. Tack stitch in place.

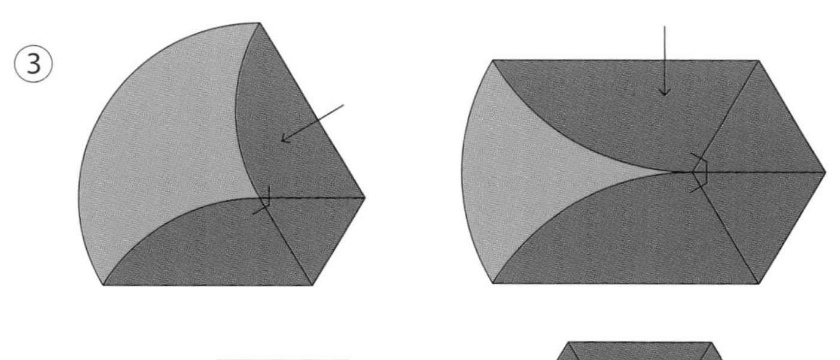

3. Continue working around the circle, folding the right corner to the center and tack stitch in place, until a six-sided shape, or hexagon, is formed.

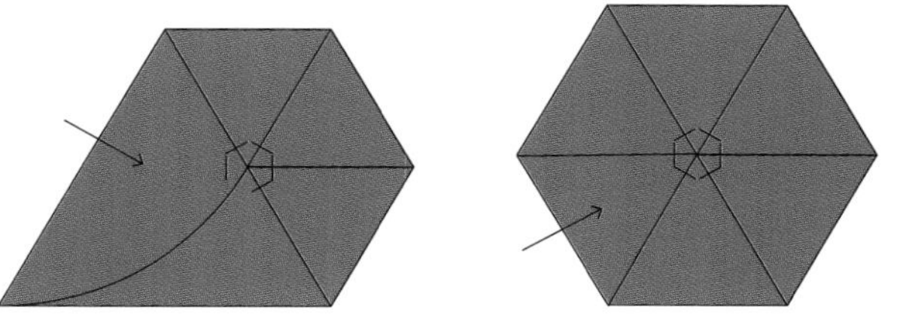

4. Repeat steps 2 and 3 with the 1½" circle. Sew the small circle onto the center of the larger circle. Stitch to background fabric by embellishing the center of the flower with Beads (page 93) or Colonial Knots (page 97)

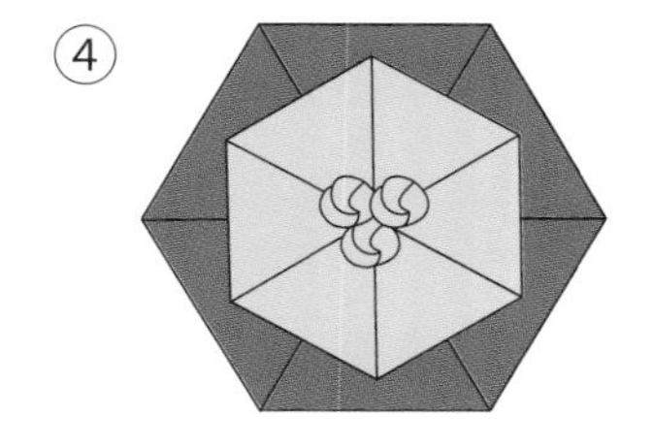

Tip *Experiment with various sizes of circles to form different sizes of flowers.*

For example, make a rose by cutting six circles, 4½", 4", 3¾", 3", 2¼" and 1½". Make a Bachelor Button from each circle. Stack one circle on top of another, large to small, offsetting corners of each hexagon. Secure together in center. Add Beads or Colonial Knots in center to complete.

the stitch

Beads

Beads add interest, dimension and sparkle to a design. They come in many shapes and sizes in a vast range of colors and materials. A fine strong needle and thread are recommended for attaching beads to fabric. A hoop is also recommended for beading.

Attaching Beads

1. Bring the needle and thread to the front at A. Slide a bead onto the needle.

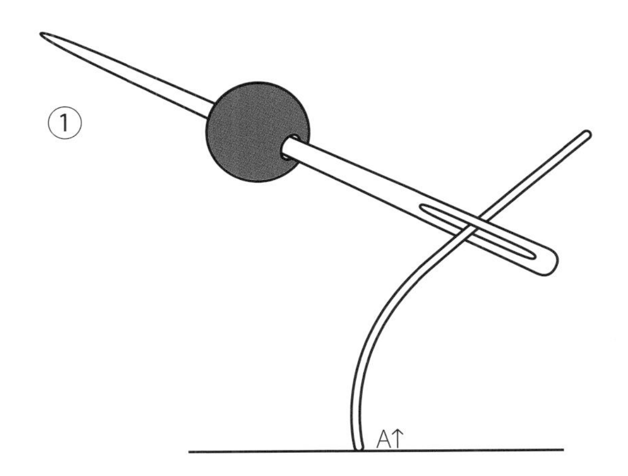

2. Slide the bead down the thread onto the fabric. Take the needle and thread to the back at B, at the end of the bead.

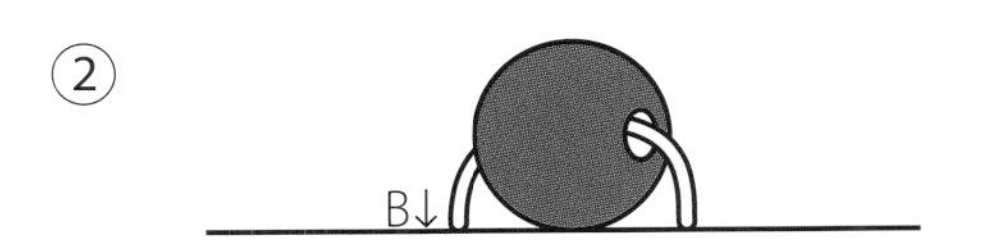

3. Bring the needle and thread to the front at A, through the bead, and down at B a second time. Secure on the back.

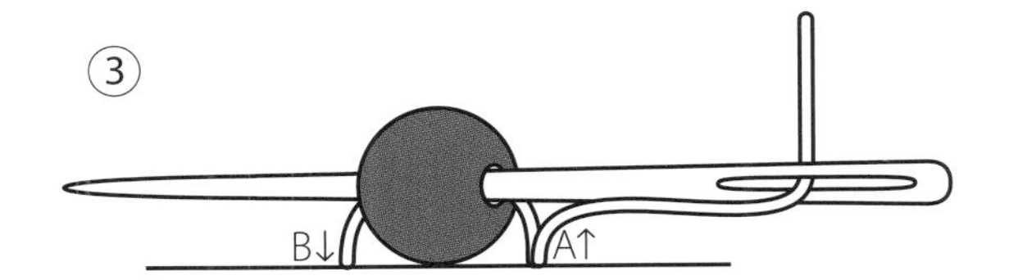

the stitch Boat Leaf

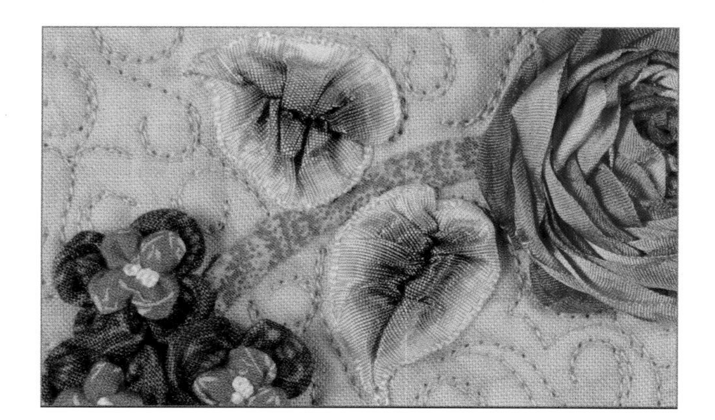

This is a versatile leaf that is easily customized simply by changing the width, length, and gathering of the ribbon or fabric. A Boat Leaf made with fabric is constructed the same way as a Boat Leaf made with ribbon. The difference is in the preparation of the fabric for making the leaf.

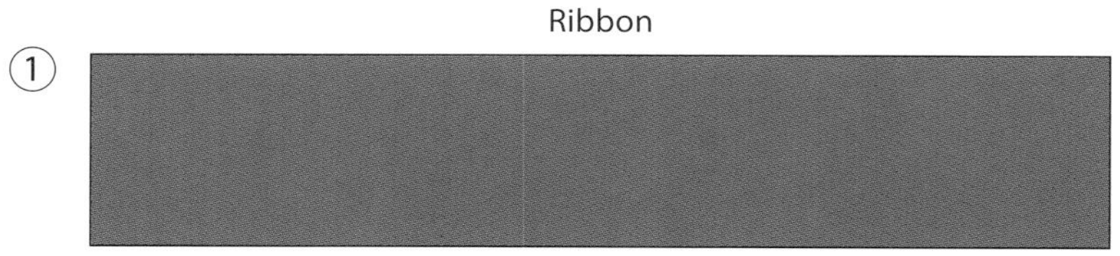

1. For a Ribbon Boat Leaf, cut a length of ribbon 7 times the width of the ribbon. Fold the ribbon in half, right to left, right sides together, matching the cut ends.

Tips

- *To change the width of the leaf, use a narrower or wider ribbon.*
- *To change the length of the leaf, cut a longer piece of ribbon to begin, i.e., 9 or 12 times the width of the ribbon.*
- *To change the fullness of your leaf, gather the ribbon looser or tighter.*

2. For a Fabric Boat Leaf, cut a piece of fabric 1" x 3¾". Fold the lengthwise edges to the center, wrong sides together. Press. Fold the fabric in half, right to left, right sides together, matching the cut ends.

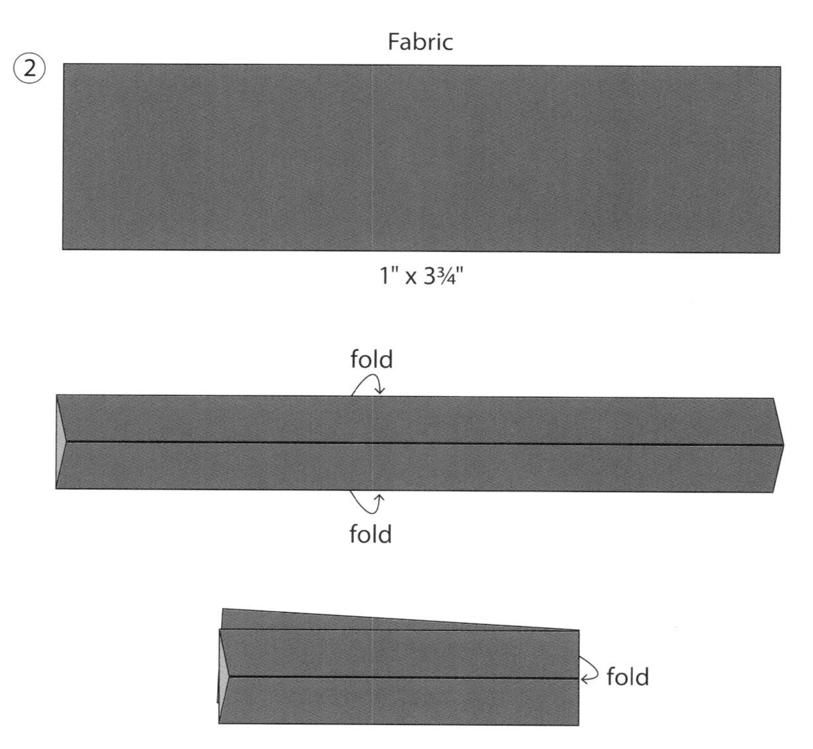

Boat Leaf *continued*

3. Fold up the two corners of the ribbon or fabric, forming what looks like a boat. The 90-degree corners are approximately 3/16" below the top edge of the ribbon or fabric. Pin in place. *Turn the boat upside down.*

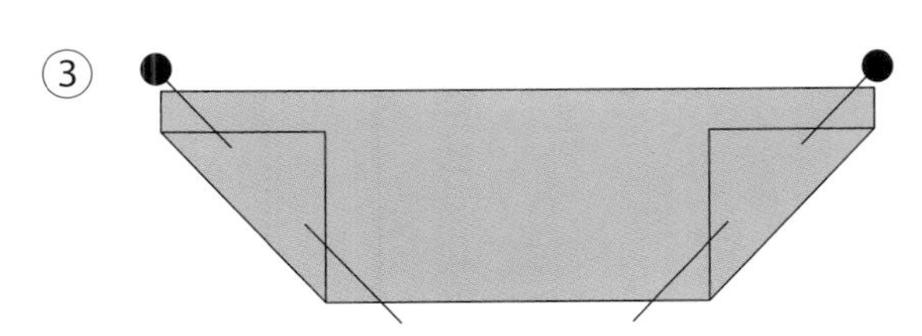

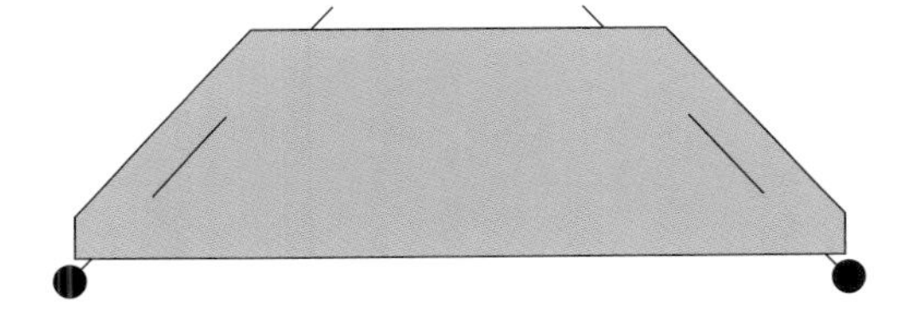

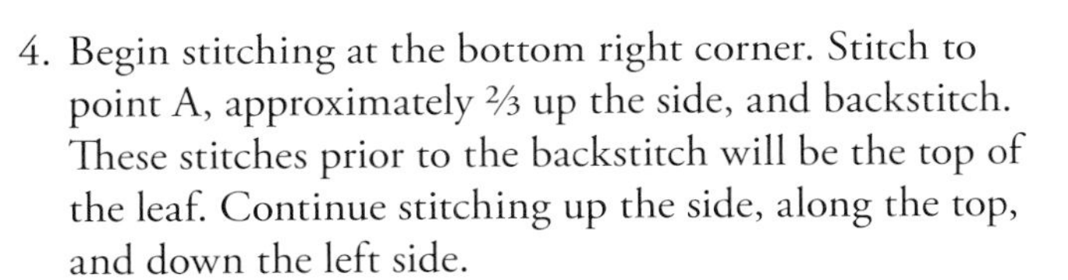

4. Begin stitching at the bottom right corner. Stitch to point A, approximately 2/3 up the side, and backstitch. These stitches prior to the backstitch will be the top of the leaf. Continue stitching up the side, along the top, and down the left side.

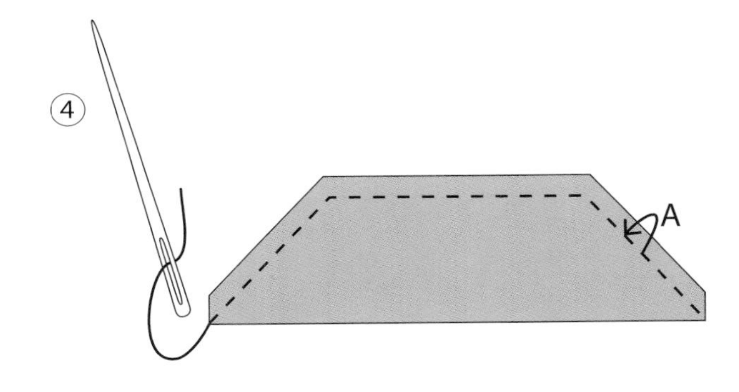

5. Gather up the stitches into the bottom of the boat. Open up the leaf, check for desired size, and then secure stitching.

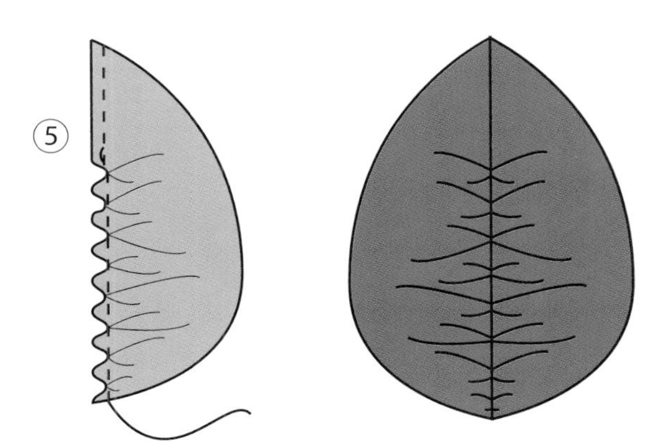

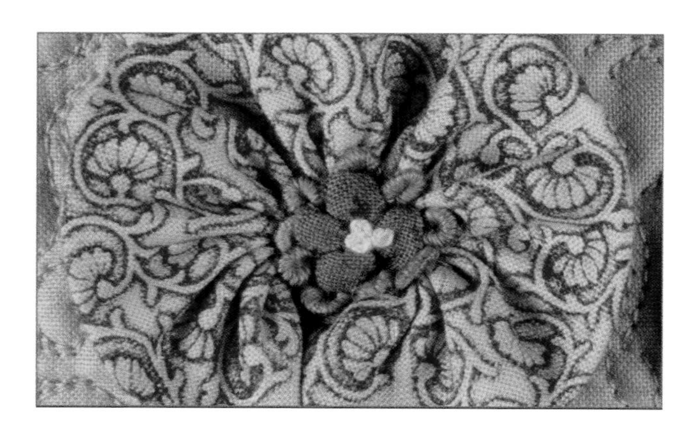

the stitch

Buillion Knot

So much can be done using this wonderful knot. Vary the threads, the length of the stitch, number of threads, or number of wraps, the finished stitches are too numerous to imagine. From buds to flowers, sepals, petals, and leaves, even butterflies, caterpillars, and snails, the possibilities are endless.

It is best to work this stitch with a Straw or Milliner's needle, since it has a consistent width the length of the needle shaft. If using crewel wool, gimp, or ribbon, a Chenille needle is suggested for its wider eye, easily accommodating the thickness of these mediums.

①

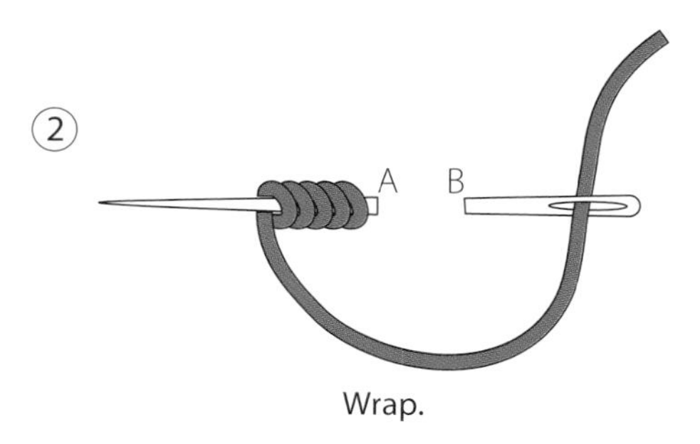

Up at A, down at B, up at A.
Leave needle in the fabric.

1. Bring the needle and thread to the front at A. Take the needle to the back at B (horizontally right of A). Bring the tip of the needle to the front at A again. Do not pull the needle all the way through the fabric.

②

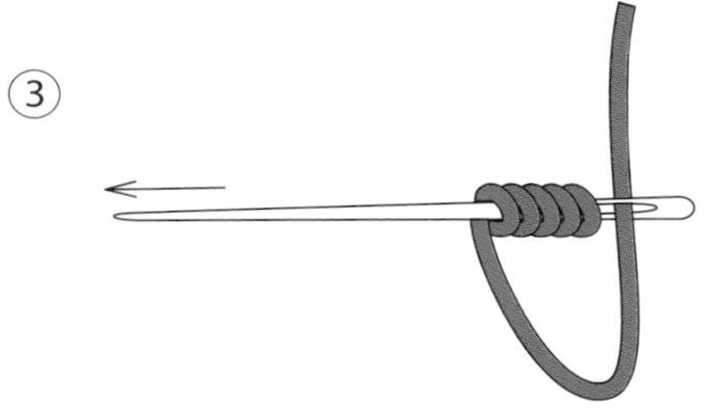

Wrap.

2. Gently wind the thread around the needle. These are referred to as "wraps". The number of wraps should cover the distance between A and B.

③

Hold wraps in place.
Pull needle & thread through the wraps.

3. Holding the wraps against the surface of the fabric with your thumb, gently pull the needle and thread through the wraps, placing the wraps on the thread. Be sure the wraps lay side by side on the top of the fabric. These wraps should cover the space between A and B.

④

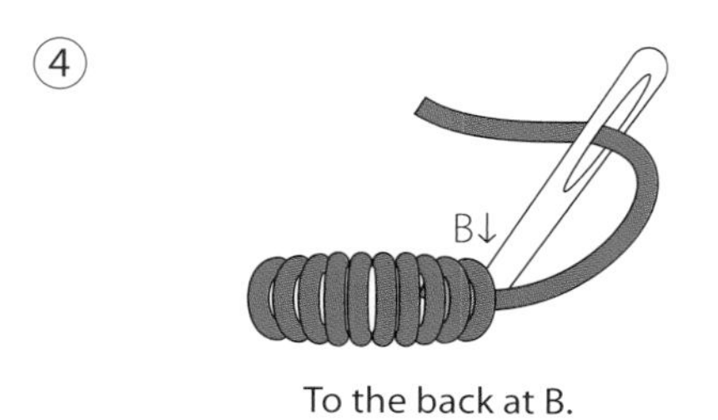

To the back at B.

4. Take the needle to the back at B. The bullion should be laying smoothly next to the fabric.

Tip *In order to obtain a gentle curve to your Bullion Knot the number of wraps should be greater than the distance between A and B. If 5 wraps nicely fill the space between A and B, add an additional 3-4 wraps for a curved effect between A and B. The gentle curve is wonderful when stitching rose buds or rose petals.*

the stitch Colonial Knot

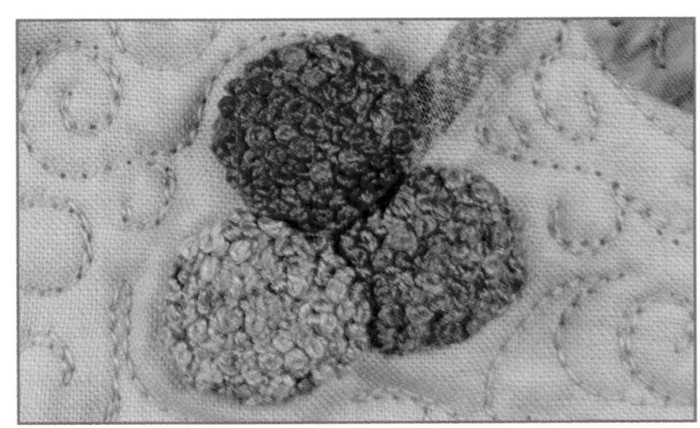

The Colonial Knot, also known as the Candlewicking Knot, is similar in appearance to the French Knot and can be worked alone or to fill a shape. It is easier to work this stitch with the fabric in a hoop. This leaves your hands free to position stitches and to wrap the thread around the needle.

1. Bring needle and thread to the front at A. Make a backward "C" with the thread. Place the tip of the needle under the top of the "C" close to A.
2. Lay the thread from the end of the "C" over the tip of the needle and shorten the loop around the needle.
3. Take the thread under the tip of the needle. The thread looks like it is forming an almost closed figure 8.
4. Take the tip of the needle to the back at B, two threads away from where the thread originally emerged at A. Pull the wrapped thread firmly against the fabric and pull the needle and thread through to the back.

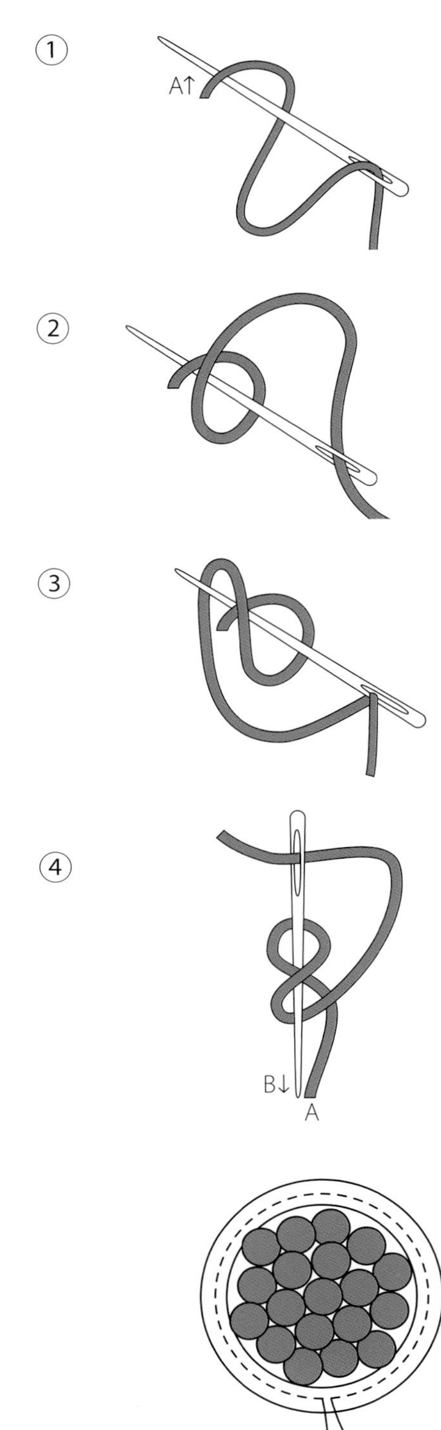

 Tip

An embellishing technique to add dimension to berries or flower centers is to make stuffed circles. Here's how:

Trace a circle on a 7" square of muslin. Place in an embroidery hoop and fill the circle with:

- *Beads (page 93)*
- *Bullion Knots (page 96)*
- *Colonial Knots (page 97)*

Run a row of gathering stitches around the outside edge of the circle. Trim leaving a 3⁄16" seam allowance. Gather and stuff with batting. Secure gathering and appliqué to the block.

the stitch Fishbone Stitch

This is a beautiful stitch for delicate leaves or use it to stitch multiple petals for a flower's star center.

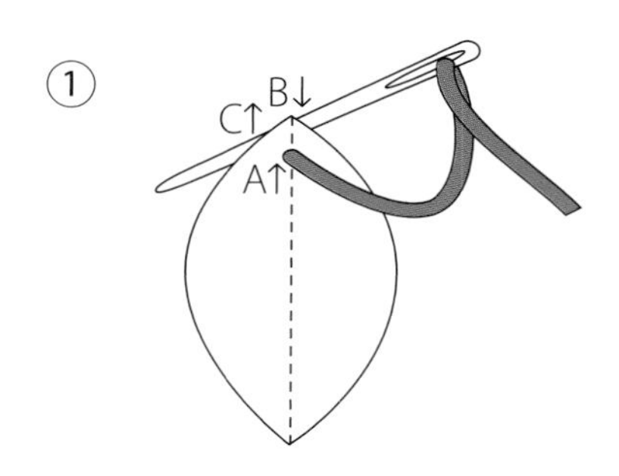

1. Lightly mark the outline of the leaf shape with a center line on the fabric. Bring the needle and thread to the front at A. Then take the needle from B to C. Make sure the thread is to the right of the needle.

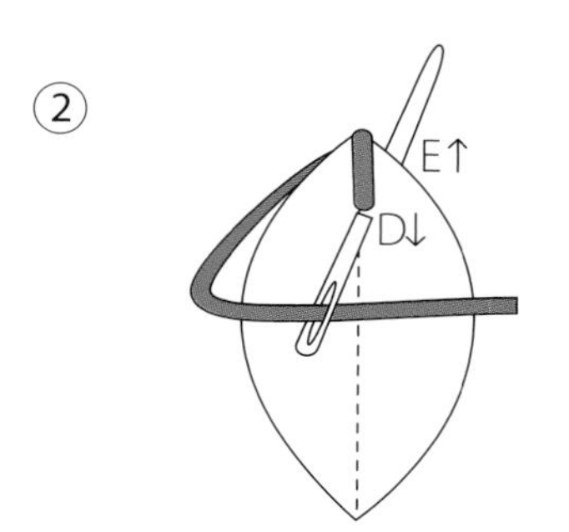

2. Pull the needle and thread through the fabric. Make sure the thread is to the left of the needle. Take the needle from D to E.

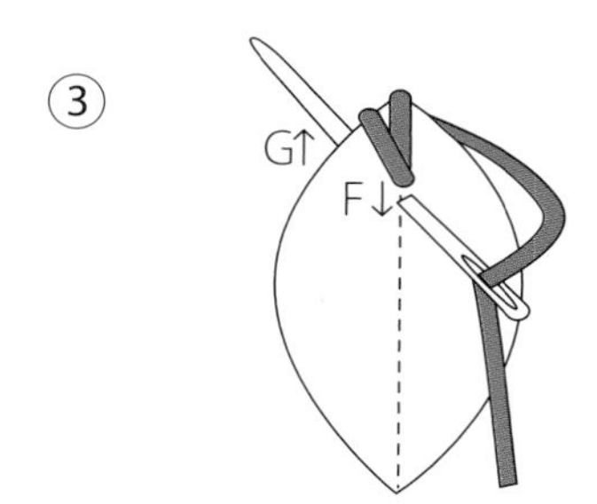

3. Pull the needle and thread through the fabric. Make sure the thread is to the right of the needle. Take the needle from F to G.

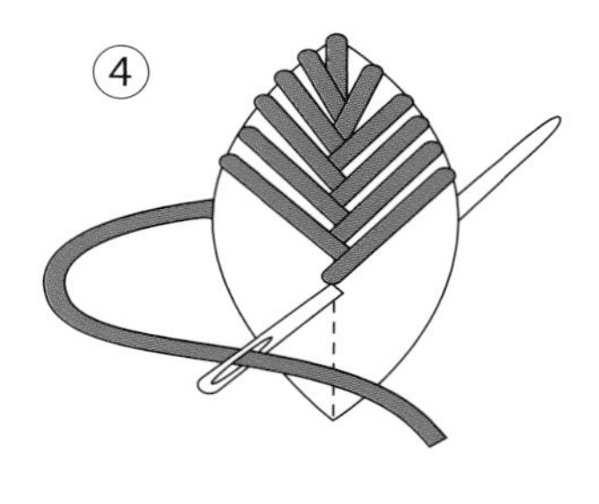

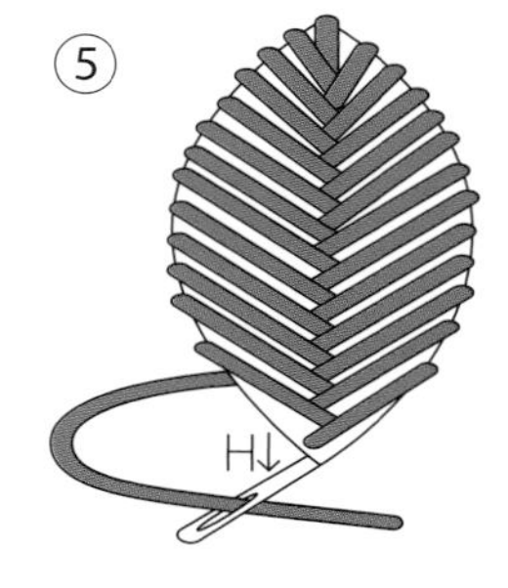

4. Pull the needle and thread through the fabric. Continue working down the leaf from side to side, following steps 2-3.

5. Finish the stitching by taking the needle and thread to the back at the bottom of the center line at H and secure on the back.

the stitch

Gathered Flowers

The basic gathered flower will blossom into a magnificient array of flowers, limited only by the width, length, colors, and types of ribbon. Work this flower in silk, wired, or grosgrain ribbon, or different fabrics such as cotton, silk, or chiffon for multiple effects. Mokuba ribbon makes an exquisitely dainty flower.

1. Cut a length of ribbon 9 times the width of the ribbon. If using wired ribbon, remove the wire from the bottom edge. The bottom edge will be the center of the flower.

   If using fabric, cut a length of fabric twice the finished width and a length 9 times the finished width. Fold the fabric in half lengthwise wrong sides together. For example 2" (finished width 1") x 9".

①

length is 9 times width of the ribbon

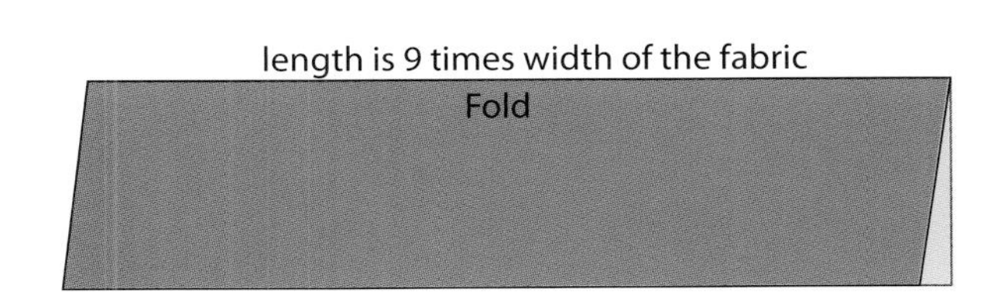

2. Secure a knotted gathering thread at A (approximately ⅛" from cut edge) with a backstitch. Stitch from A to B along the sides and bottom edge of the ribbon or fabric, curving the stitching line at each corner.

②

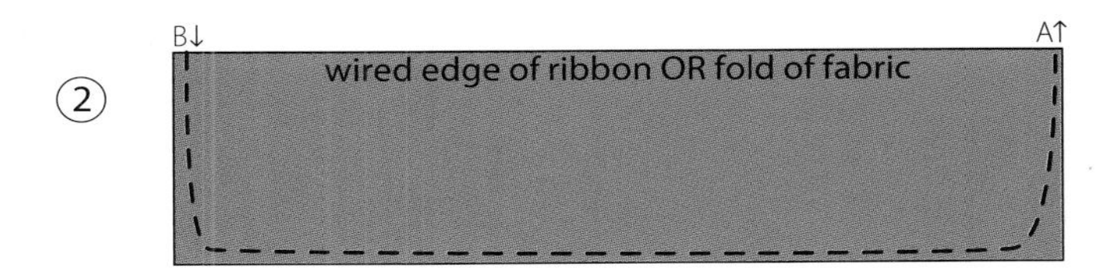

3. Draw up the gathers to approximately ½". Backstitch and knot the thread at B to secure the gathering. Do not cut the thread.

③

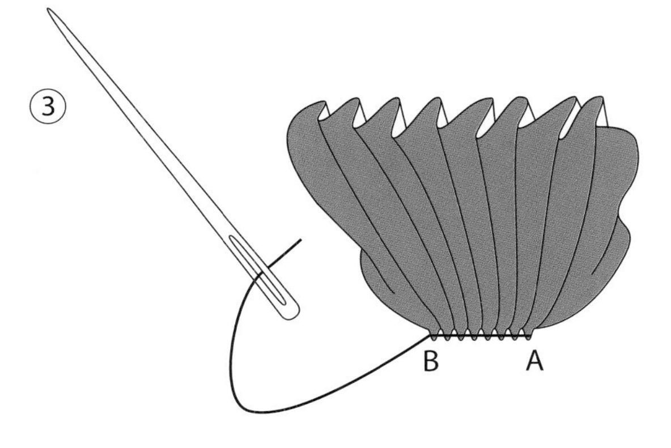

4. Form the ribbon or fabric into a circle, overlapping the ends. Secure both layers together in the center (not at the top outer edge), hiding the securing stitches in a gathered fold.

④

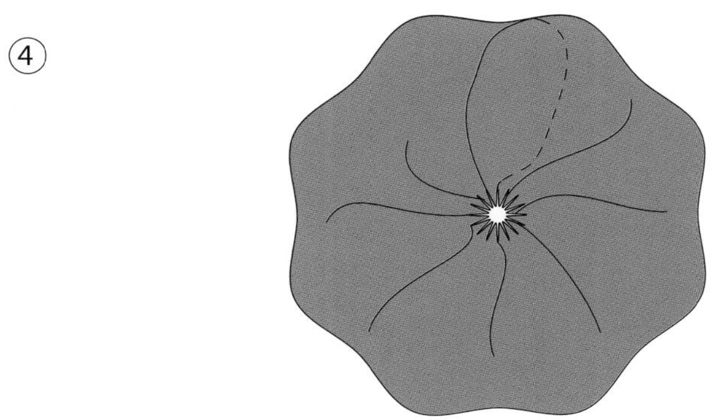

Tips

- *For a more ruffled edge, cut a length of ribbon or fabric up to 14 times the width of the ribbon.*
- *Cut a length of ribbon or fabric 30 times the width of the ribbon or fabric. As you gather the ribbon or fabric, allow it to spiral around its center, overlapping the "rows". Adjust the gathers to obtain the desired effect.*
- *Instead of forming the basic Gathered Flower into a circle, form it into an open arc to use as a bud. You can even layer 2 or 3 of these "arc" flowers on top of each other behind a calyx for a pompon effect.*

the stitch Jan's Ruched Rose

Ruching is an ancient sewing technique used to gather a strip of fabric or ribbon to form scallops or petals. In Jan's Ruched Rose, the distances are varied between sections of petals allowing the flower to bloom as it is stitched. This flower can be made with both fabric and ribbon, offering endless possibilities.

A **fabric flower** is made with a 1¼" x 33" piece of fabric. Fold both lengthwise edges toward the center, wrong sides together, and press. The finished width of the strip is ⅝".

A **ribbon flower** is made with a ⅝" x 33" piece of wired ribbon. Removed the wire from the bottom edge of the ribbon. The remaining wired edge will be the top edge of the flower.

1. Mark the top and bottom edges of the fabric or ribbon as stated below the diagrams.

2. Cut a 36" piece of cotton thread. Fold it in half and thread the needle. Knot the thread. Using the marked dots as a guide for stitching a "V" pattern, bring the needle and double stranded thread to the front at A and stitch down to B, up to C, down to D, and so on until five mountain tops are formed.

① 18–1¼" 8–¾" 5–½" ¼"

top edge

Place a dot ¼" from the top right side edge.
From the dot: mark 5–½" increments
mark 8–¾" increments
mark 18–1¼" increments

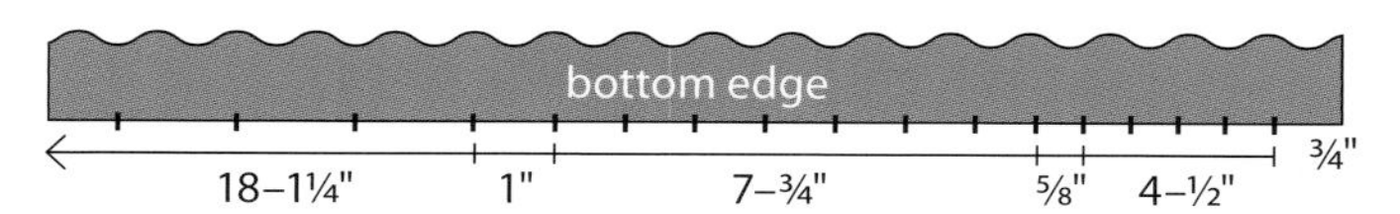

Place a dot ¾" from the bottom right edge.
From the dot: mark 4–½" increments
mark 1–⅝" increment
mark 7–¾" increments
mark 1–1" increment
mark 18–1¼" increments.

Trim the left edge of the fabric or ribbon ¼" from the last marked dot on the bottom edge.

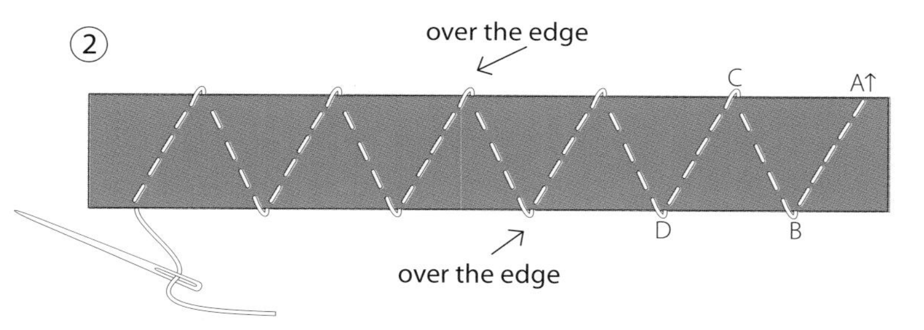

 Tip

Looking at the first valley point (B), if the needle and thread go down to the back at the bottom of the valley, bring the needle and thread over the edge and resume stitching going down on the front and working up to the mountain top (C).

Looking at the first mountain top point (C), if the needle and thread come up on the front at the top of the mountain, bring the needle and thread ***over the edge*** *and resume stitching coming up from the back and working down to the valley (D).*

Making this loop over the edge of the fabric or ribbon at the peaks and valleys forms the petals when the thread is gathered.

Jan's Ruched Rose *continued*

3. Gently gather the fabric or ribbon on the stitches forming petals. Once gathered, the stitching line will run through the center of the fabric or ribbon, with petals on the top and bottom of the stitching line. Knot the thread at this point to secure the gathers.

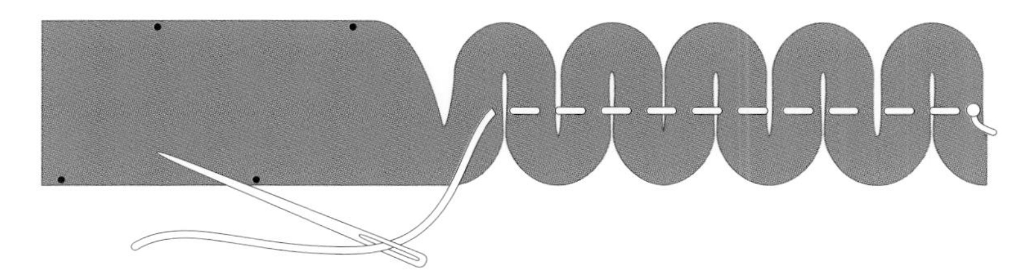

4. Work four more mountains, gather, and knot; four more mountain tops, gather, and knot. You will notice the next 8 petals are slightly taller than the first five petals.

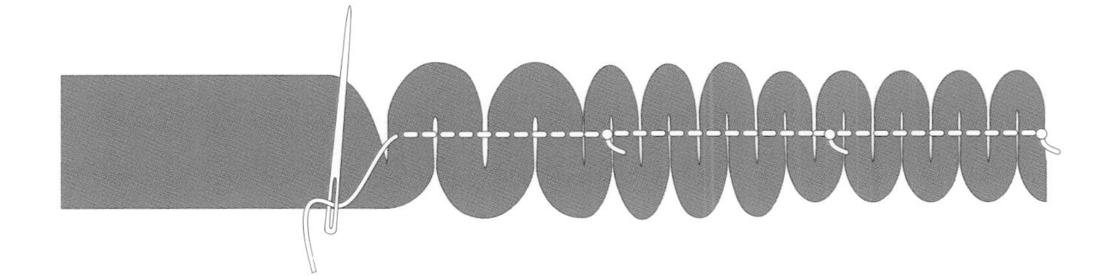

5. Continue working across the length of the fabric or ribbon until all the petals are formed.

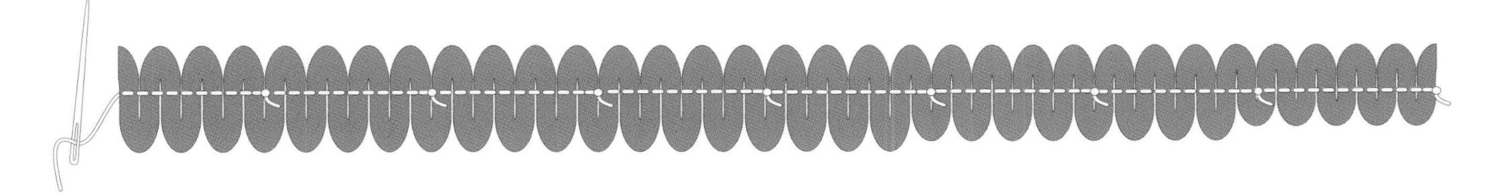

6. Double thread a new needle. Bring the needle from back to front in the first five bottom petals.

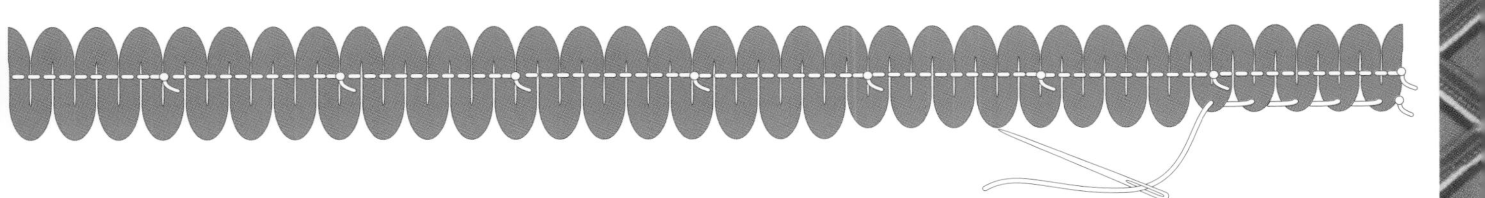

Jan's Ruched Rose *continued*

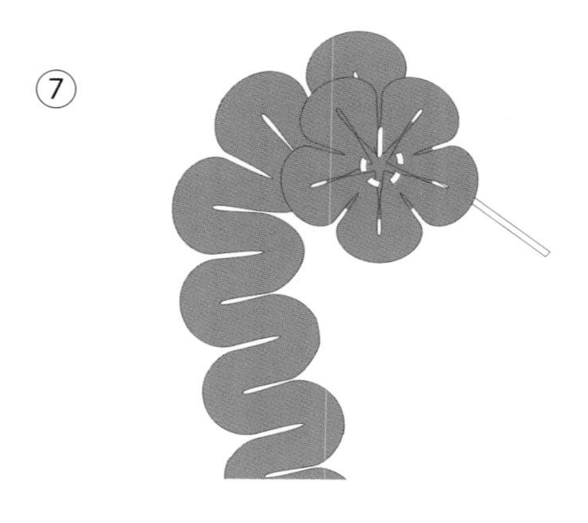

7. Pull the thread through the lower five petals to gather. Knot to secure the gathers. Place the first and fifth petals right sides together. Tightly wrap the working thread several times between the petals and secure. Open the five petals flat revealing the flower center. DO NOT CUT the thread after knotting.

8. Continue to wrap the petals around and behind the flower center, trying to offset the mountain tops. Every two to three petals, secure the petals to the previous round of petals with tiny stitches, hiding the stitches in the folds of the gathered petals.

9. Continue working the petals around the flower to the desired finished size. Angle the end of the ribbon to the back of the flower and secure.

the stitch

Mitered Leaf

The Mitered Leaf is a simple leaf that will quickly add dimension to an appliquéd block. It works up beautifully with ribbon or fabric.

1. Cut a piece of ribbon 1" x 4" OR a fabric strip 2" x 4". If using fabric, fold the strip in half lengthwise, wrong sides together, forming a 1" x 4" fabric strip.

   Fold the ribbon or fabric in half lengthwise to 1" x 2".

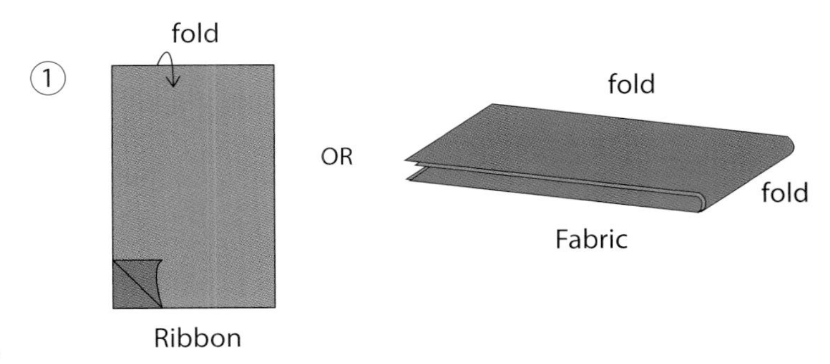

2. Fold the top left corner of the ribbon or fabric down at a 90-degree angle. Stitch close to the folded edge. Trim away triangle. Open the leaf.

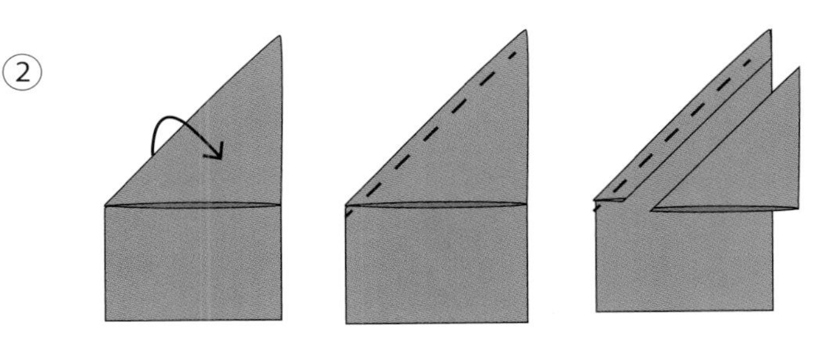

Tip *Start stitching a stitch length away from the top edge. When the leaf is opened, the point will be crisper.*

3. On the right side of the ribbon or fabric, baste along the bottom edge. Gather, forming and shaping the leaf as desired. Knot and secure gathering in place. Stitch the opening closed in the center seam line.

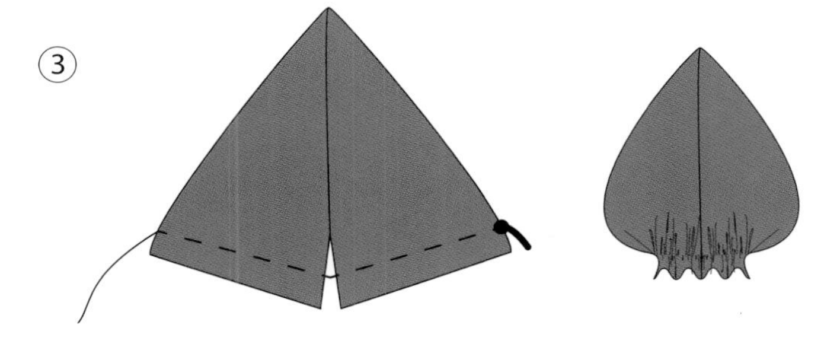

4. Tuck the bottom raw edge up and under the leaf and secure. Appliqué the leaf in place.

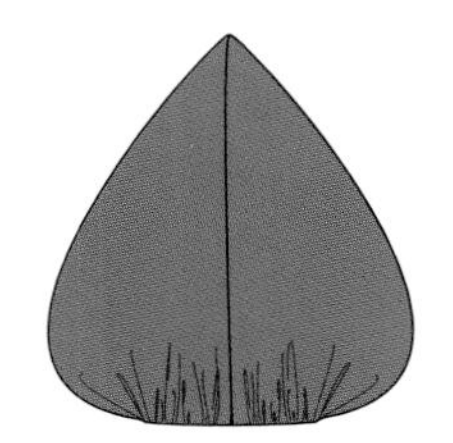

the stitch

Petal Flower

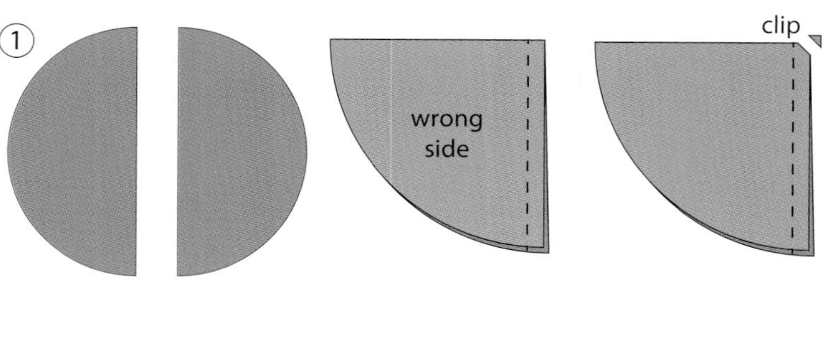

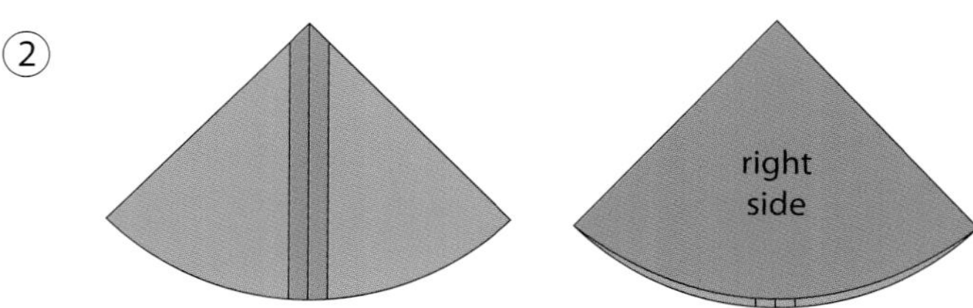

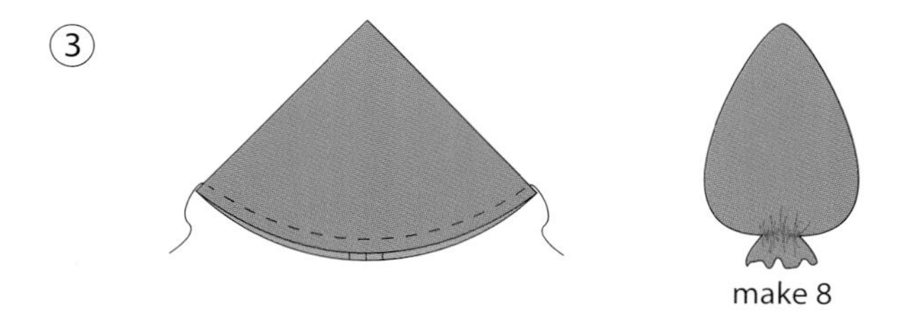

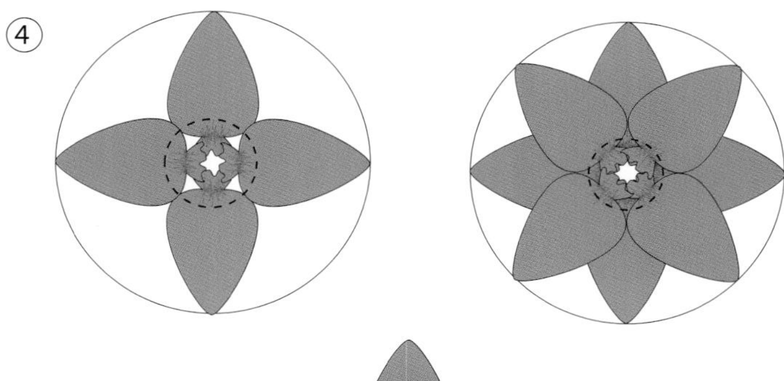

This little eight-petalled fabric flower is easy to make. It offers a nice dimensional effect on any block and could be layered with larger petals in the back. Experiment with various size circles to achieve your desired result.

1. Cut four 2¼" circles. Cut each circle in half to make eight half circles. Each half circle will be one petal.

   Fold a half circle in half, right sides together, matching straight edges. Sew the raw straight edges together with an ⅛" seam allowance. Clip the seam allowance at the top fold just short of the seam line.

2. Finger press the seam allowance open and turn the petal right side out, centering the seam on the back.

3. Join the two bottom edges together with a running stitch. Pull to gather and secure. Make 8 petals.

4. Trace a 2" circle on a 7" x 7" piece of muslin. Place in a 5" embroidery hoop. Place four petals north, south, east and west, with the tip of each petal on the outer edge of the traced circle. Pin in place. Sew the petals in place along the bottom edge of each petal.

   Place the four remaining petals diagonally between the four secured petals. Sew in place along the bottom edge of each petal.

5. **Flower Center** – Make a single Traveler's Joy (page 114) using a 1½" circle. Secure to the center of the Petal Flower with Colonial Knots (page 97). Remove from the embroidery hoop and trim away the muslin. Position on block and secure in place.

the stitch

Pistil Stitch

The Pistil Stitch is a combination stitch made up of a French Knot on the end of a Straight Stitch. It is perfect for making flower stamens and petals.

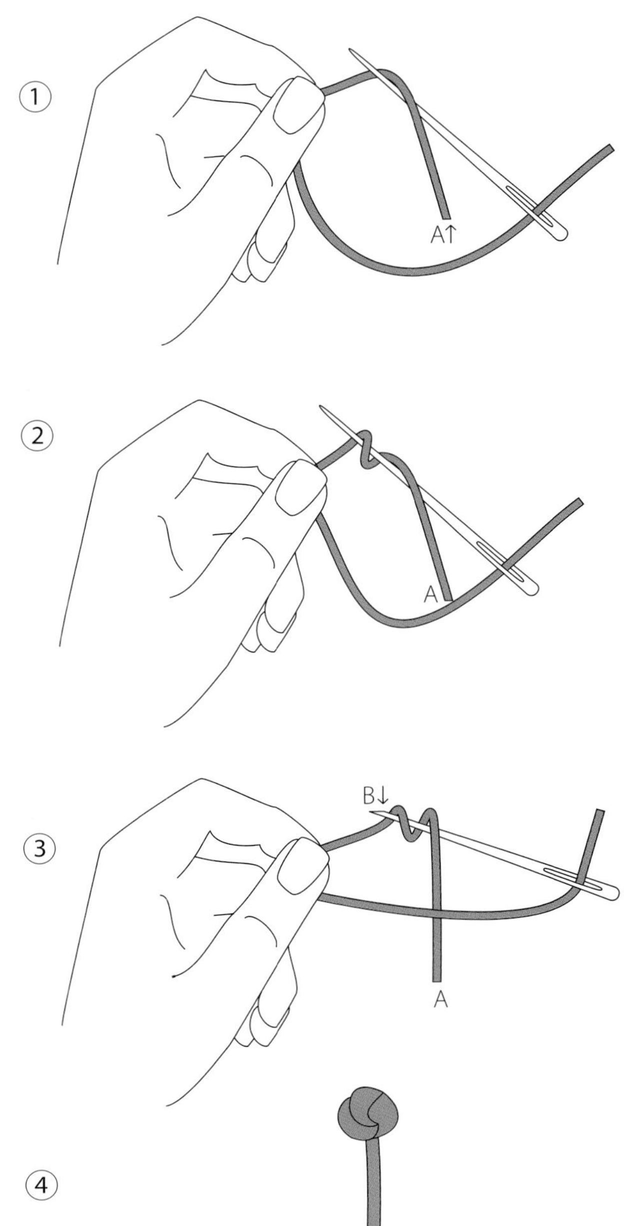

1. Bring the needle and thread to the front at A (the base of the Straight Stitch).

2. Holding the working thread firmly with your left hand, bring the thread over the needle. Wind the working thread counterclockwise around the needle the desired number of wraps (two wraps are illustrated).

3. Holding the thread taut, place the tip of the needle in the fabric at B (the end of the Straight Stitch).

4. Slide the wraps down the needle onto the fabric. Pull the needle and thread through the fabric to form the French Knot on the top of the Straight Stitch.

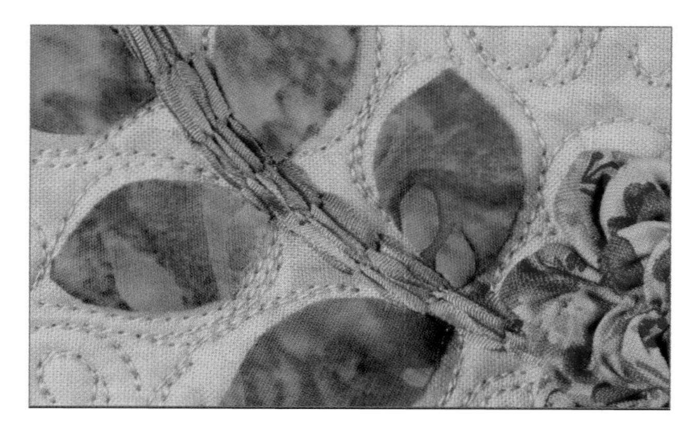

the stitch Raised Stem Stitch

The Raised Stem Stitch is a great filling stitch. It is created from a foundation of Straight Stitches upon which rows of Stem Stitches are worked. A Crewel needle is suggested for the foundation stitches, and a Tapestry needle for the Stem Stitch. When using this stitch to fill an uneven area, an outline of Stem Stitches may be used to smooth the edges.

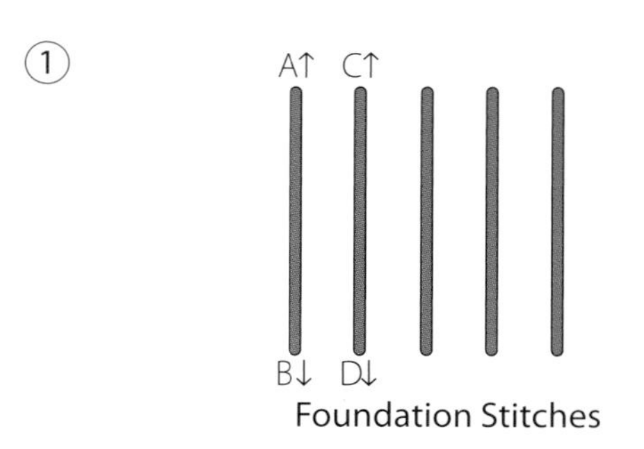

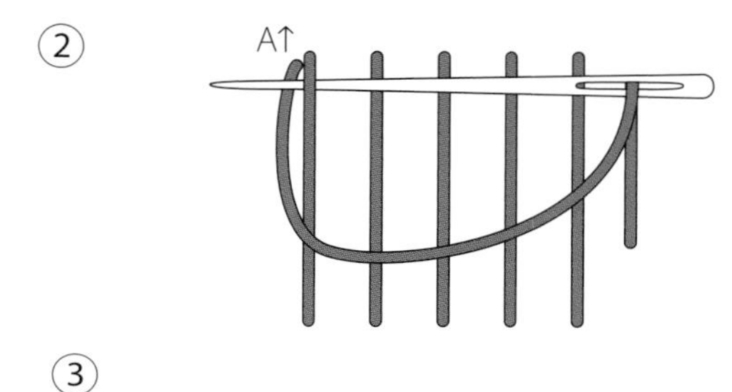

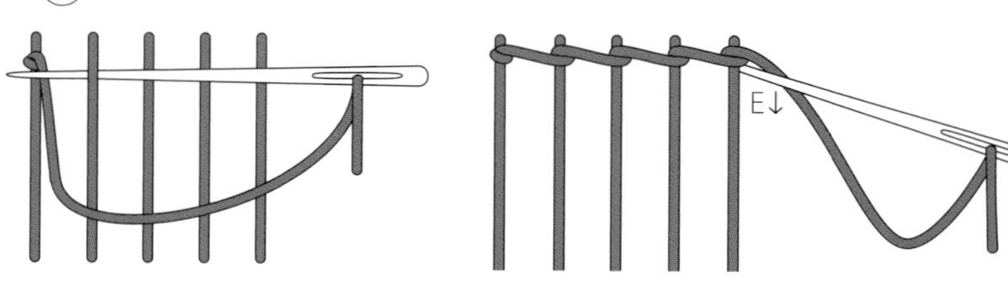

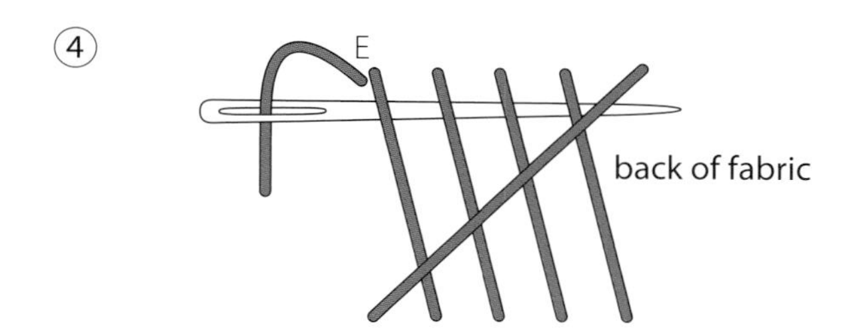

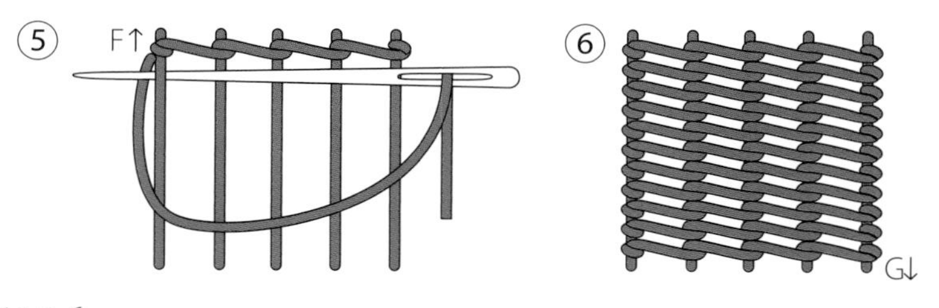

1. Foundation: Draw the design on the right side of the fabric. Work rows of parallel Straight Stitches (page 113) at right angles to the drawn design. Bring the needle and thread up at A, down at B, up at C, down at D, and so on.
2. Raised Stem Stitch: Bring the needle and thread to the front at A. Keeping the working thread below the needle, take the needle and thread under the first Straight Stitch, right to left. Do not pierce the fabric. Pull the working thread upward until the thread is wrapped firmly around the Straight Stitch. The first Raised Stem Stitch is made.
3. Keeping the working thread below the needle, take the needle and thread under the second Straight Stitch, right to left. Pull the working thread upward until the thread is wrapped firmly around the Straight Stitch. The second Raised Stem Stitch is made. Proceed in this manner across the line of Straight Stitches. At the end of the row, use the tip of the needle to gently pack the stitches down. Take the needle and thread to the back at E.

Tip *Be careful not to pull the Stem Stitches too tightly, pulling the Straight Stitches inward.*

4. On the wrong side of the fabric, slide the needle and thread under and across the Straight Stitches to the opposite side.
5. On the right side, bring the needle and thread to the front at F, just below A.
6. Repeat Steps 2-5 until the design is filled and the Straight Stitches are covered. At the end of the last row, take the needle and thread to the back at G and secure.

the stitch Ribbon Stitch

This is one of the most versatile stitches for ribbon embroidery. It is perfect for leaves, stems, calyxes, and flower petals. The shape of the stitch is determined by the width of the ribbon, stitch length, insertion point at the end of the stitch, and the tension on the ribbon when the needle is pulled through the needle.

1. Bring the needle and ribbon to the front of the fabric at A. Lay the ribbon on top of the fabric and insert the needle in the middle of ribbon at B.

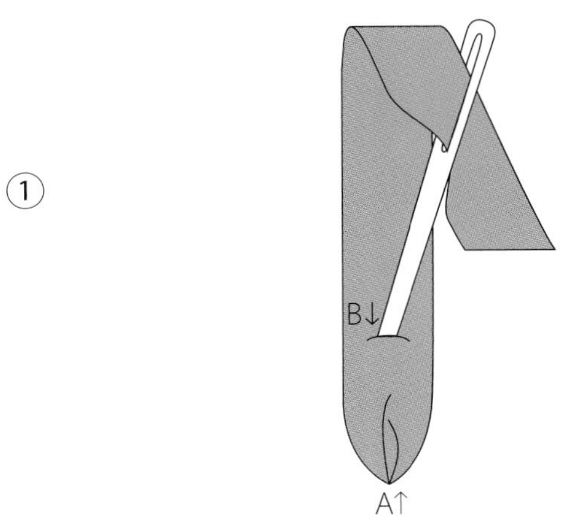

2. Take the needle and ribbon to the back, gently pulling the ribbon through until the ribbon folds back on itself at the tip and the ends of the ribbon curl inward.

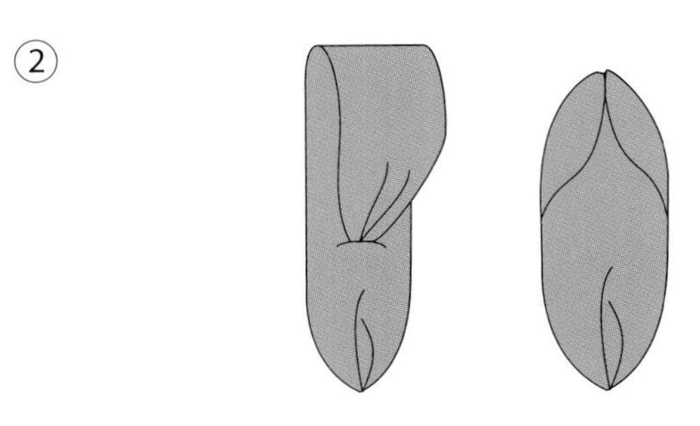

3. This is a perfect stitch to create leaves. By inserting the needle to the left or right of center at B, the ribbon will curl to the right or left, forming a leaf.

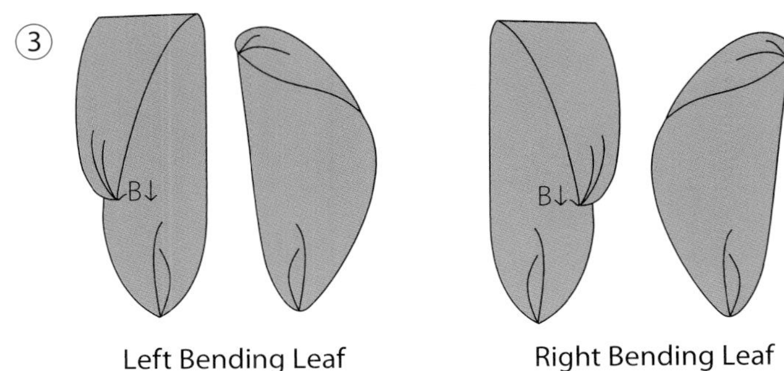

Left Bending Leaf

Right Bending Leaf

Additional techniques using the Ribbon Stitch may be found in the book "The Art of Elegant Hand Embroidery, Embellishment and Appliqué" by Janice Vaine.

the stitch Round Ruched Rose

The Round Ruched Rose is a beautiful fabric flower. It is made with circular ruching, working the mountain/valley stitching in a circle. You will always be delightfully surprised at the floral results you can achieve with different fabric and prints. Small or large, this flower is sure to please.

①

3" x 3" OR 5" x 5"

1. Cut a 3" x 3" square of fabric for a small rose or a 5" x 5" square of fabric for a large rose.

②

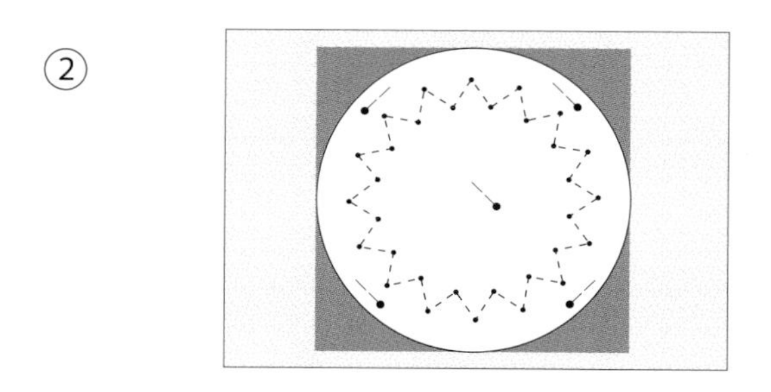

2. Place fabric right side up on a flat surface.
   Place transfer paper on top of the fabric with the graphite side down.
   Trace the pattern on page 109 and cut out.
   Place it right side up on the transfer paper and pin the three layers together.
   Using a stylus, TRACE THE CIRCLE and MARK ONLY THE DOTS.
   Remove pins.
   Cut out the fabric circle on the drawn line.

③

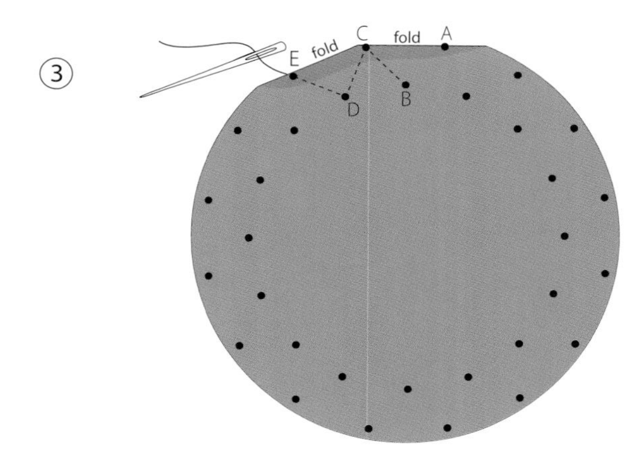

3. Working from the right side of the circle, fold the fabric to the back between A and C.
   Bring a needle and double knotted thread to the front at B. Stitch to C.
   Fold the fabric to the back between C and E. Stitch from C to D, then D to E. As you stitch the "V", catch the fabric folded to the back.

④

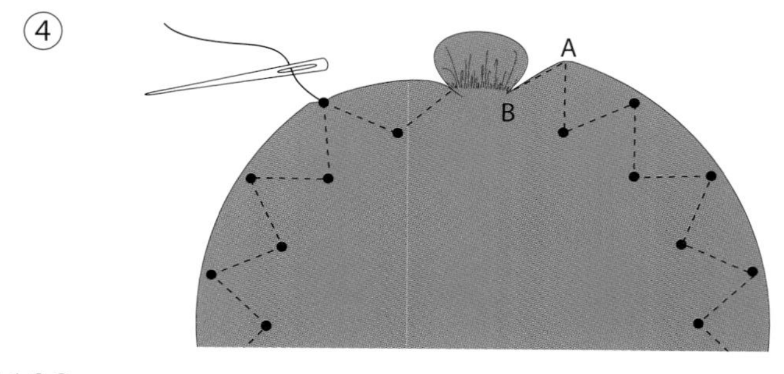

4. Gather the stitching and the petals of your flower will begin to form.
   Continue working around the circle, folding the fabric to the back, stitching the "V" and pulling to gather.
   After you have completely stitched around the circle, finish by stitching down to B, the point of beginning.

Round Ruched Rose *continued*

5. Gather but DO NOT KNOT at this point. Loosen or tighten the gathered petals as needed to form a 1" circle for the small flower or a 2" circle for the large flower. Adjust the petals to make them all the same size. Now secure the gathered stitching.

   Gently push the center of the ruched rose flat.

   Secure the rose to the fabric with a small straight stitch hidden in the folds of each petal. Tack the center to create beautiful dimension.

Tips

- *I place the flower under a heavy object for a time to "press" the ruched center.*
- *Embellish the flower center with Colonial Knots (page 97), Pistil Stitches (page 105), Straight Stitches (page 113), Beads (page 73), or a small Traveler's Joy (page 114). You could also place a small Round Ruched Rose in the center of the large rose.*

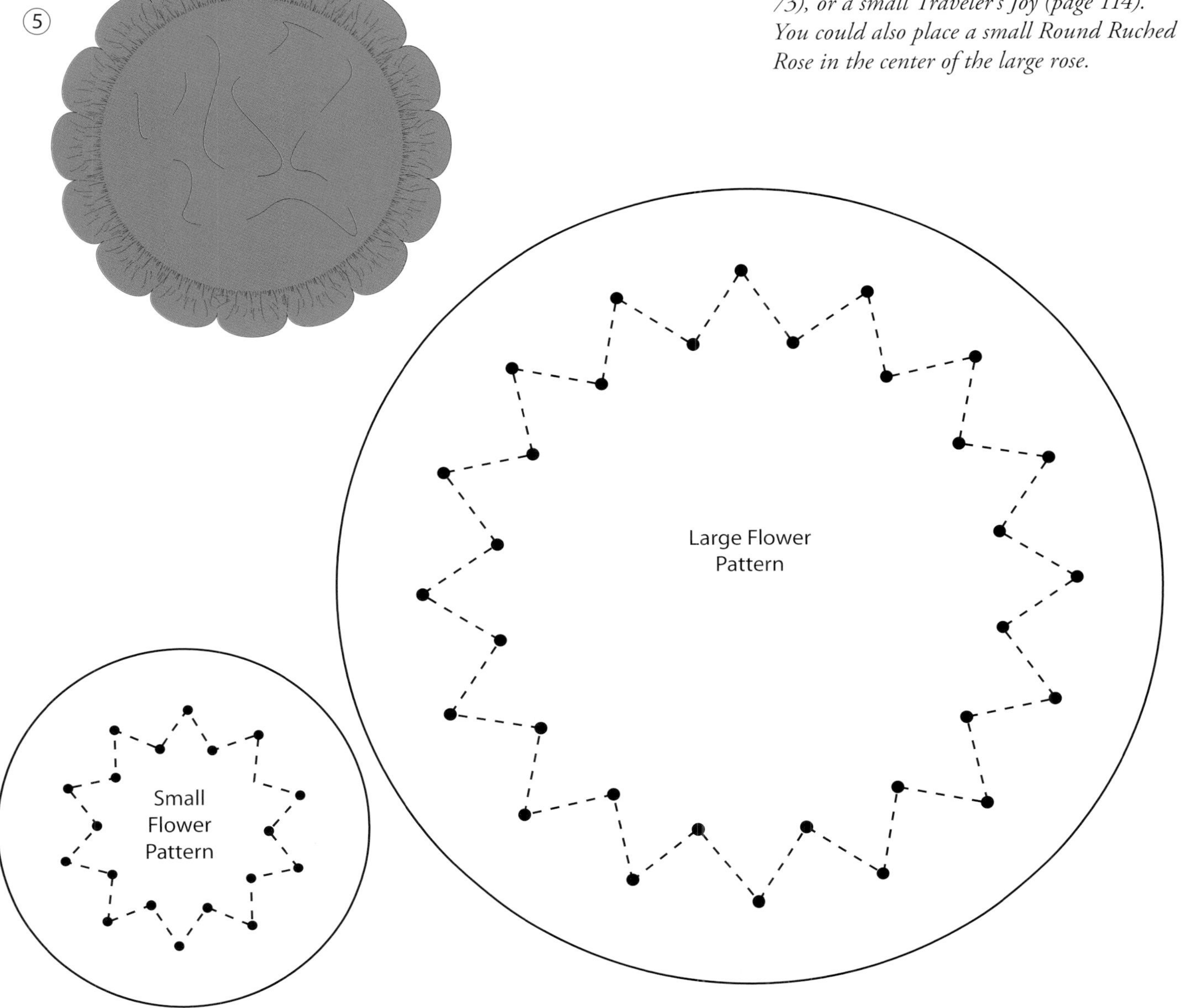

the stitch Spider Web Rose

The Spider Web Rose is a versatile stitch that can be made with thread, ribbon, and fabric to produce different yet equally exquisite effects. This textured stitch is created by weaving the thread, ribbon or fabric through a foundation of odd numbered Straight Stitch spokes. The larger the rose, the greater number of spokes, always odd numbered.

The Foundation (work on wrong side of fabric)

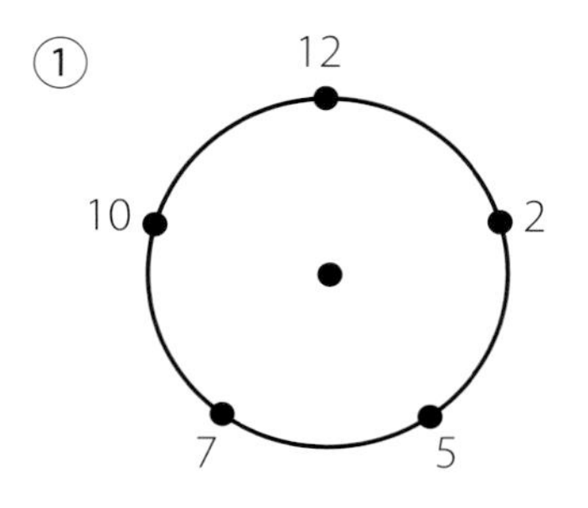

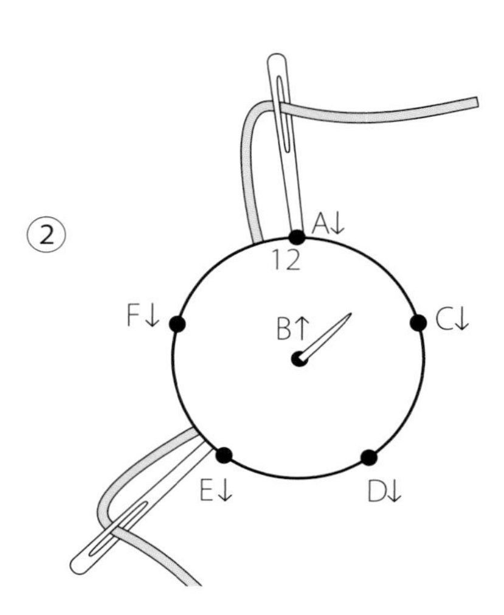

The Foundation

1. Lightly draw a circle on the wrong side of the fabric. Dot the center and the outer points of the five spokes. Mark the spokes at 12, 2, 5, 7, and 10 o'clock.

Tips

- *Use a Perle Cotton No. 5 or No. 8 to work the spoke foundation in a color matching the thread, ribbon or fabric of the Spider Web Rose.*
- *To make a bigger circle, increase the number of spokes. The number of spokes should always be an odd number.*

2. Still working on the wrong side of the fabric, take a knotted thread and needle down at A and up at B. Continue working around the circle going down at C and up at B; down at D and up at B; down at E and up at B; down at F and up at B, forming a 5-spoke wheel on the right side of the fabric. Secure thread on the back.

Finished 5-spoke wheel (right side of fabric)

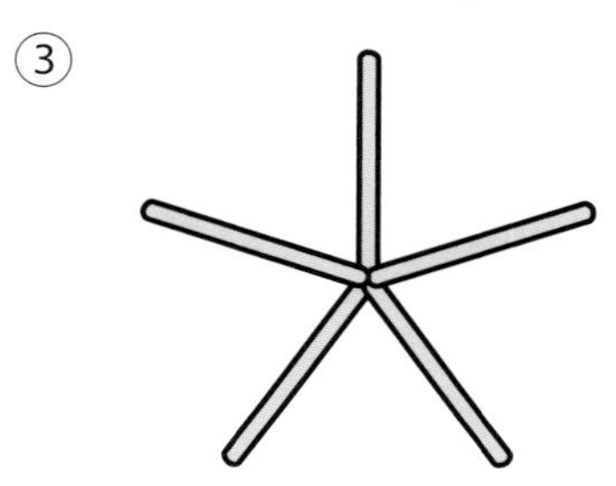

3. When you turn the fabric over to the right side, a 5-spoke wheel has formed. This will be the foundation for the Spider Web Rose.

Spider Web Rose *continued*

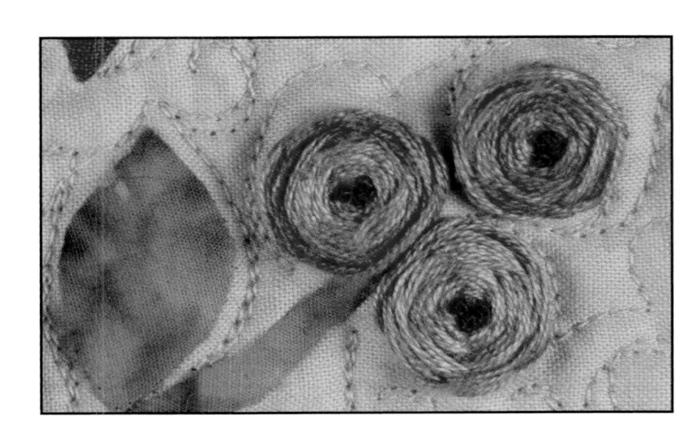

The Rose (work on right side of fabric)

The Rose

1. Bring the needle and thread or ribbon to the front between two spokes as close as possible to the center. If using a fabric tube*, stitch the beginning of the tube on the right side between two spokes.

   Working in a counter-clockwise direction, weave the thread, ribbon, or fabric over and under the spokes until one round is complete. Pull firmly so the spokes do not show at the center. Work 2 more rounds in the same manner.

2. Slightly loosening the tension as you work consecutive rounds, weave the thread over and under the spokes, working to the outer edge until the spokes are completely covered. Allow the thread, ribbon, or fabric to gently twist as you weave around the spokes. The rose should lay on top of the fabric without pulling or distorting the foundation. Take the needle and thread or ribbon to the back and secure. If using a fabric tube, tuck the end of the fabric under the outer edge of the rose and tack in place.

①

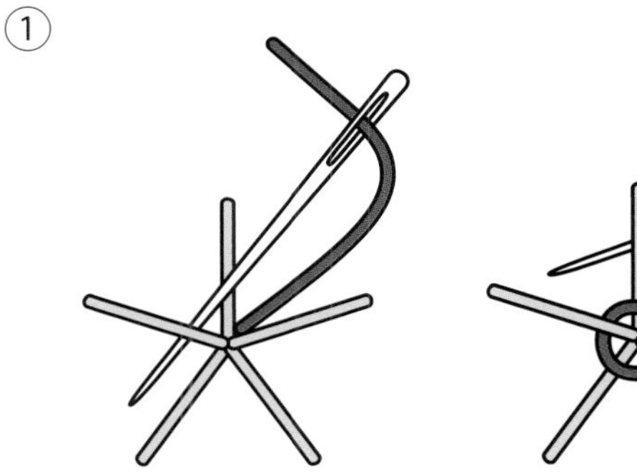

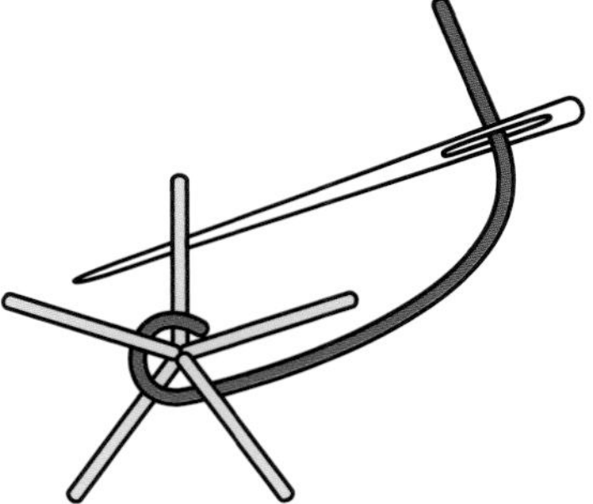

②

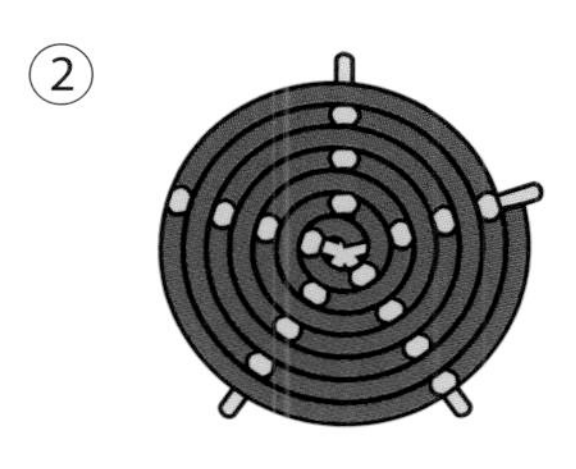

Thread

Ribbon or Fabric

Tip

With each round, alternate the thread, ribbon or fabric over and under a spoke. If you are going over a spoke, or under a spoke, twice in consecutive rounds, a stitch has been missed. Be sure the under and over stitches alternate with each round.

*A fabric tube is made with a 1" x 42" strip of fabric sewn right sides together with a ¼" seam allowance down the length of the strip. Easily turn this strip with a *Skinny Mini Tube Turner by Mary Kay Perry Designs*™.

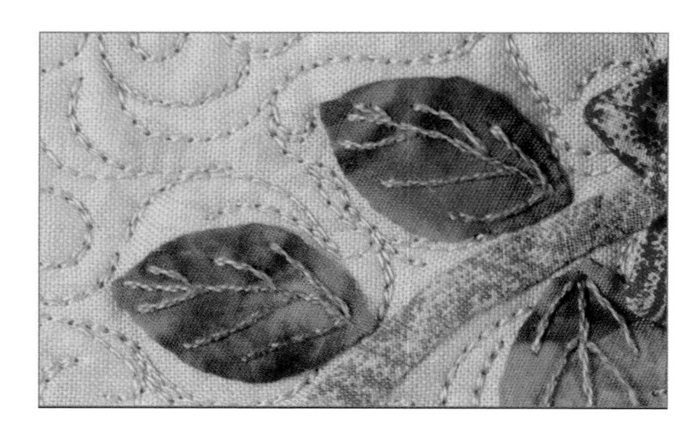

the stitch

Stem Stitch

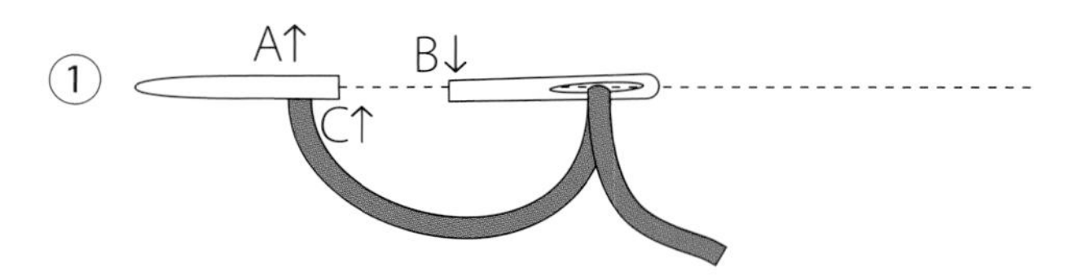

The name, Stem Stitch, describes its purpose. Choosing the right thread or ribbon can make the perfect fine stems. Stitch several rows of Stem Stitches side by side to make a thicker stem for a flower or tiny branch. Experiment with 2, 3, or 6 strands of floss and 2mm, 4mm, or 7mm silk ribbon to see the beautiful effects this basic embroidery stitch has to offer.

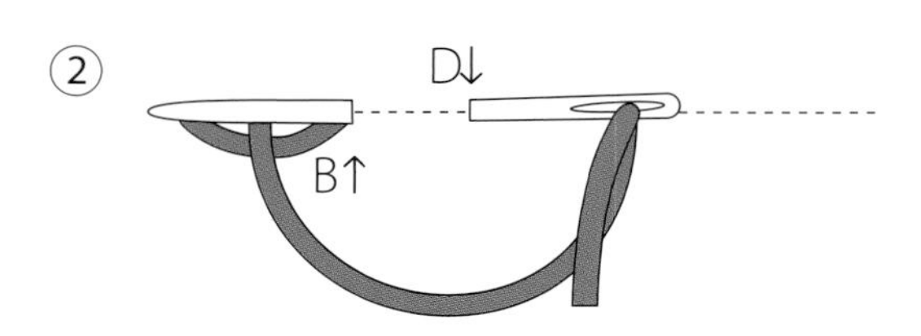

1. Lightly mark a line on the fabric. Bring the needle and thread to the front at the left end of the line at A. With the working thread below the needle (swings low), take the needle to the back at B and up at C between A and B.

2. Pull the needle and thread through the fabric. Again with the thread below the needle (swings low), take the needle down at D and up at B.

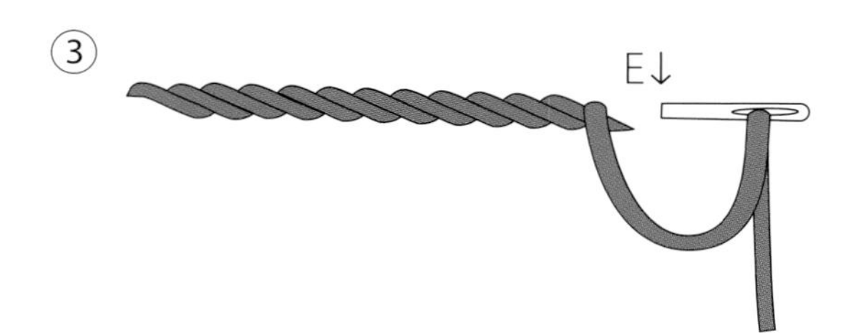

3. Following step 2, continue working stitches in the same manner across the line. Always keep the thread below the needle. To end, take the needle and thread to the back at E for the last stitch. Secure on the back.

Tips

- *The Stem Stitch takes curves beautifully and will work well for embellishing the wreaths in this book. When working a curve, such as on the wreaths, keep stitches small so the line remains smooth around the curve.*
- *The Stem Stitch made with a single strand of cotton embroidery floss creates a defining touch as the veins on a leaf.*

the stitch

Straight Stitch

The Straight Stitch is the most basic of all embroidery stitches. It may be stitched in any length and worked in any direction, vertically, horizontally, or diagonally. It is the foundation of many embroidery stitches, and is often combined with other stitches, such as the Pistil Stitch on page 105.

1. Bring the needle and thread to the front at A. Take the needle and thread to the back at B. Bring the needle and thread to the front at C and down at D. Continue for the desired number of stitches.

Tips

- *Alternate long and short Straight Stitches to form a star.*
- *Work Straight Stitches in a double circle with Colonial Knots (page 97) in the center to form a flower.*

Stab Stitch vs. Sewing Method

The Straight Stitch may be formed using one of two methods, the Stab Stitch or the Sewing Method. These methods may also be applied to other embroidery stitches.

The Stab Stitch Method is taking the needle and thread to the back of the fabric (down at A), and pulling the thread all the way through to the back, then bringing the needle and thread to the top of the fabric (up at B), and pulling the thread all the way through.

The Sewing Method takes the needle from front to back to front in one continuous motion (down at A and up at B), and then pulls the thread all the way through the fabric. This method may save time, but is not recommended for keeping stitches uniform, especially for satin type stitches where the stitches need to lie consistently side-by-side.

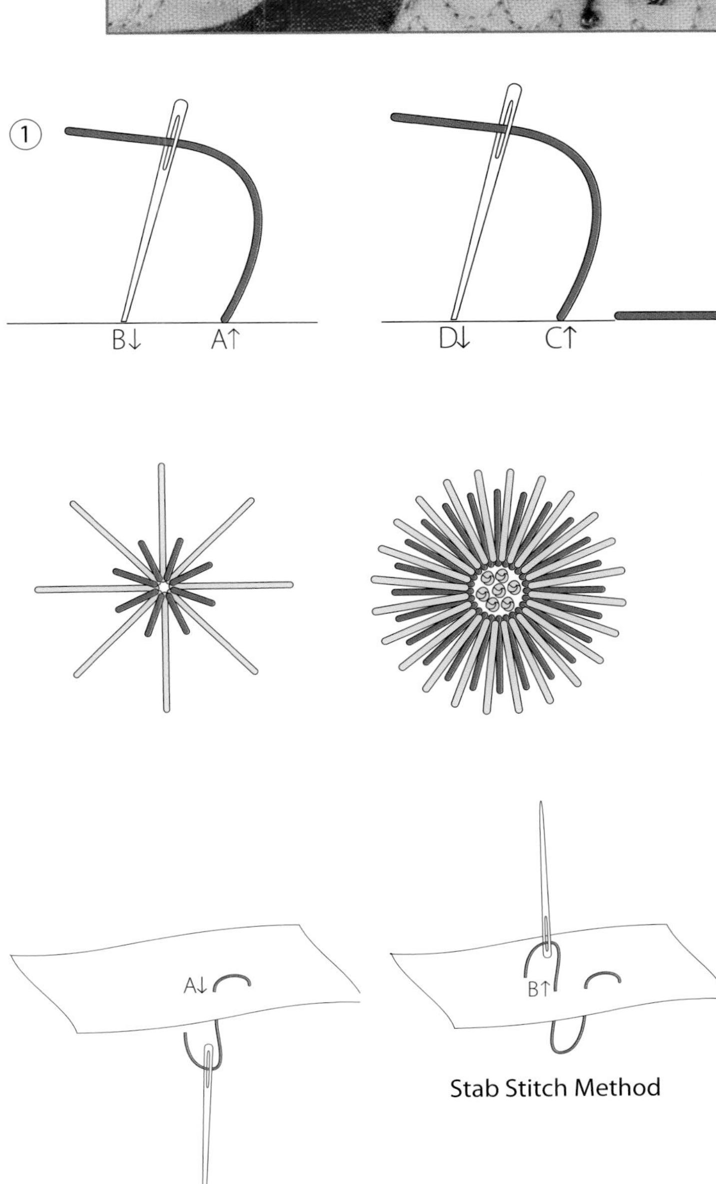

Stab Stitch Method

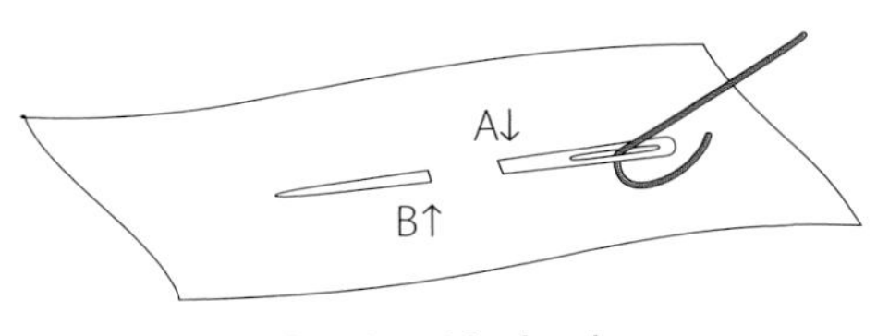

Sewing Method

the stitch Traveler's Joy

This little flower is a combination of two flowers, one placed on top of another. It may also be worked individually with a smaller circle, making tiny blossoms for lilacs or hydrangeas.

①

1. Trace a 1½" and a 2¼" circle onto the right side of the fabric. Cut out the circles, adding a 3⁄16" seam allowance.

②

2. Placing the thread knot on the wrong side of the fabric, run a gathering stitch along the traced line of the 2¼" circle. Pull the thread, gathering it tightly in the center of the circle. Knot to secure the gather. Flatten the gathered circle.

③

B

E A D

C

3. On the right side of the gathered circle, place a dot at A (center of circle), B, C, D, and E (north, south, east and west).

Traveler's Joy *continued*

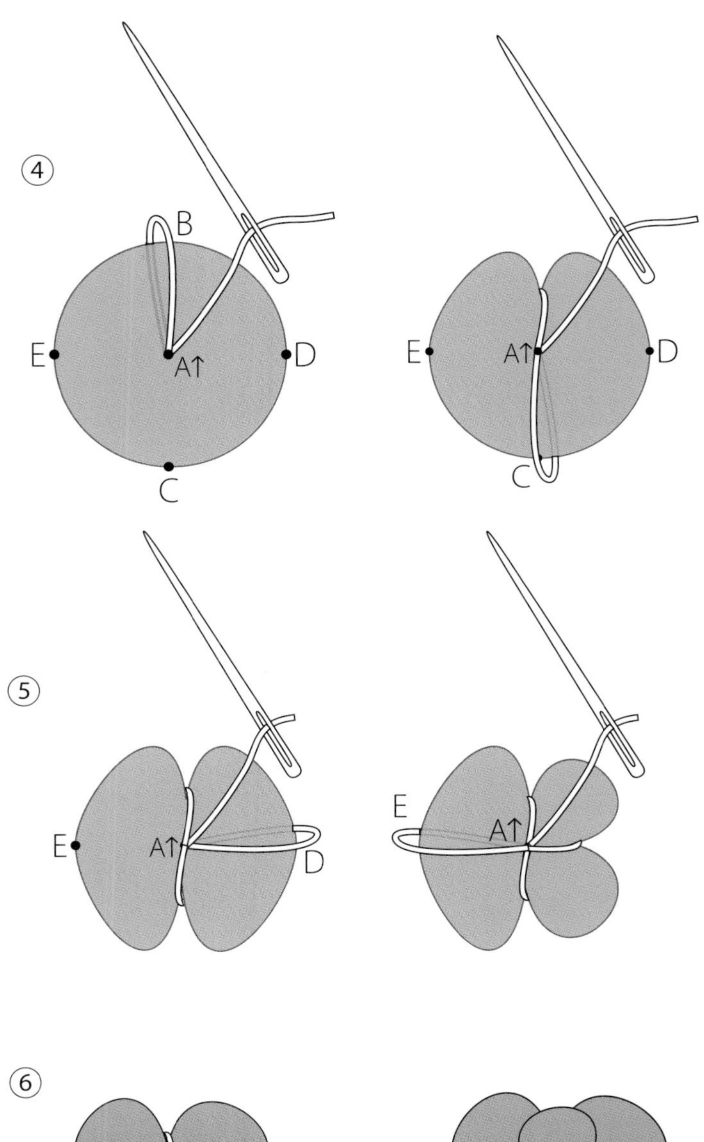

4. Bring the needle and thread to the front at A. Lay the thread over B and bring the needle and thread back up at A. Place your thumb over the thread and pull tightly making a petal indentation. Repeat a second time.

   Lay the thread over C and bring the needle and thread back up through A. Place your thumb over the thread and pull tightly making a petal indentation. Repeat a second time.

5. Lay the thread over D and bring the needle and thread back up through A. Place your thumb over the thread and pull tightly making a petal indentation. Repeat a second time.

   Lay the thread over E and bring the needle and thread back up through A. Place your thumb over the thread and pull tightly. Repeat a second time. Knot and secure. The lower flower is made.

6. Repeat Steps 2-5 for the 1½" circle. Do not cut the thread after this second flower is made.

   Place the small flower on top of the larger flower, taking the needle and thread through the center of the larger flower. Knot and secure the two flowers together.

   Attach the Traveler's Joy to the background fabric with a Bead (page 93) or Colonial Knot (page 97) in the center of the flower.

Projects

"My Mother taught me
how to sew
And at the time
I did not know
That with every stitch
I now complete
with every row
I do so neat
My Mother's heart
is there with me
Guiding my hand for all to see."
-A Sampler by Sarah, 1893-

Now that you have become proficient in needleturn appliqué and fundamental embroidery and embellishment techniques, the following pages offer several projects to display your new skills.

The Alphabet Sampler quilt, pictured on page 116, features the entire collection of alphabet blocks from pages 38-89. A Christmas quilt uses the letters "JOY" to brighten the holiday season. Four additional one-block projects are also included. You will find a smaller version of the "A" is for Appliqué Pillow, as well as a lavender sachet, a needle and pin keeper, and a small single block quilt. These one-block projects make the perfect gift for that special someone who will appreciate your labor of love.

Enjoy!

by Jo Ann Cridge, Sonnie Cridge, Luella Dusek, Gena Holland, and Janice Vaine
Quilted by Marilyn Lange

Alphabet Sampler

Quilt is 89" x 89" finished.

Fabric requirements

Appliqué Background	3¼ yards
Sashing fabric	1⅛ yards
Background	2½ yards
1st Inner Border	½ yard
2nd Inner Border	⅝ yard
Final Border	1⅝ yards
Binding	⅞ yard
Backing	8½ yards
Appliqué	Fat Quarters as desired
Embellishment	Ribbons, embroidery floss, beads as desired

Cutting

Appliqué Background:
9–12" x width of fabric strips
subcut 25–12" x 12" squares

Sashing:
19–1¾" x width of fabric strips

Background:
7–7" x width of fabric strips
7–3¼" x width of fabric strips
set aside 5 strips
from the remaining strips
subcut 4–3¼" x 4½" rectangles
6–3¼" x 9½" rectangles
1–4½" x width of fabric strip
subcut 6–4½" x 7" rectangles

1st Inner Border:
7–2" x width of fabric strips
sew strips together
subcut 2–2" x 71½" strips
2–2" x 74½" strips

2nd Inner Border:
8–2" x width of fabric strips
sew strips together
subcut 2–2" x 74½" strips
2–2" x 77½" strips

Final Border:
8–6½" x width of fabric strips
sew strips together
subcut 2–6½" x 77½" strips
2–6½" x 89½" strips

Binding:
9–2½" x width of fabric strips

Use ¼" seam allowances.

1 Appliqué Squares:

(A) Appliqué and embellish the A through Y blocks found on pages 38–87. Use the suggested stitches and supplies or choose your own variations.

(B) Press and trim each block to 9½" x 9½" as described on page 34.

2 Sashing:

(A) Sew 1–3¼" x width of fabric Background and 1–1¾" x width of fabric sashing strip together. Press away from the Background. Make 5 strip sets. Cut the strip sets into 8–12" x 4½" segments for Sashing A and 8–9½" x 4½" segments for Sashing B.

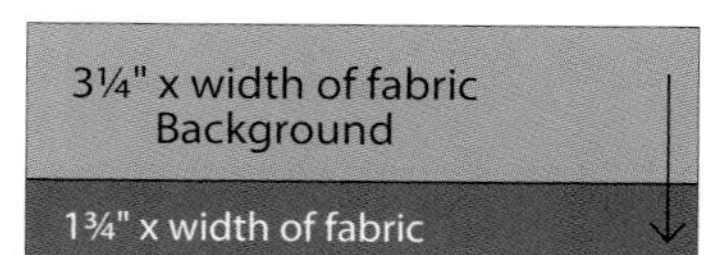

Make 5 strip sets.

Sashing A
Make 8
12" x 4½"
with seams.

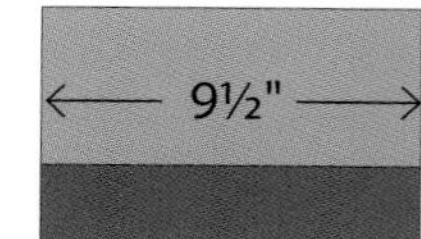

Sashing B
Make 8
9½" x 4½"
with seams.

(B) Sew 1–7" x width of fabric Background and 2–1¾" x width of fabric sashing strips together. Press away from the Background. Make 7 strip sets. Cut the strip sets into 6–10¾" x 9½"segments for Sashing C and 18–9½" x 9½" segments for Sashing D.

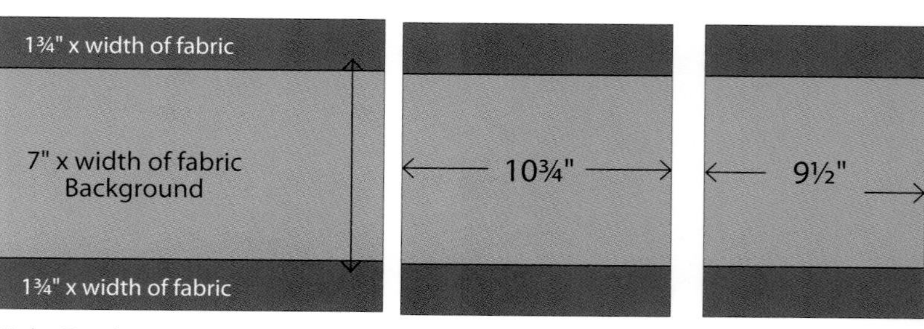

Make 7 strip sets.

Sashing C
Make 6
10¾" x 9½"
with seams.

Sashing D
Make 18
9½" x 9½"
with seams.

3 Assemble the blocks into rows as shown. Sew the rows together. Arrows show the pressing directions. Add the borders in the following order pressing away from the quilt center.

(1) 1st Inner Border –2" x 71½" strips to the sides
–2" x 74½" strips to the top and bottom

(2) 2nd Inner Border–2" x 74½" strips to the sides
–2" x 77½" strips to the top and bottom

(3) Final Border–6½" x 77½" strips to the sides
–6½" x 89½" strips to the top and bottom

4 Sew the 9–2½" x width of fabric binding strips together. Layer, quilt and bind.

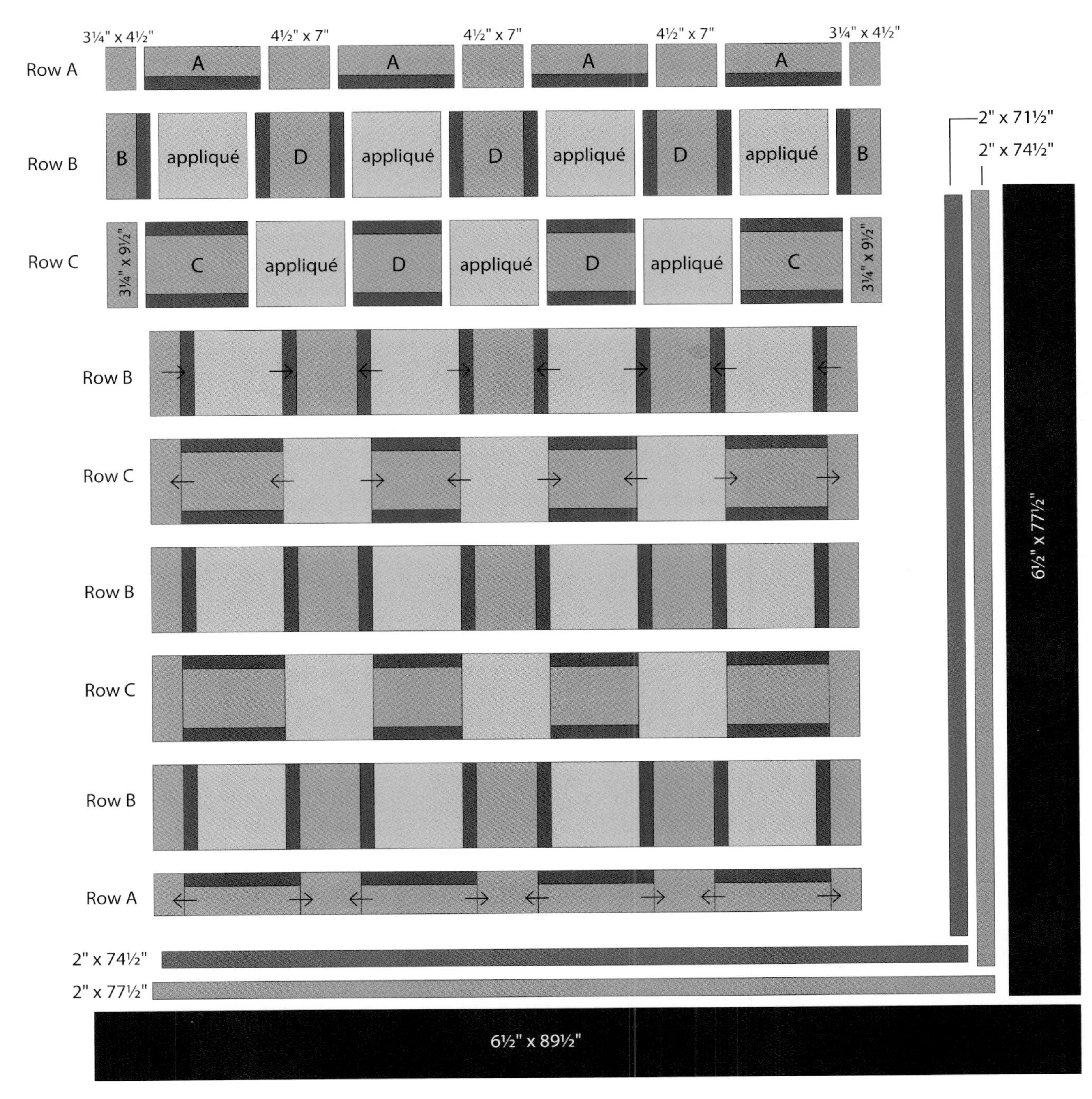

Quilt is 89" x 89" finished.

Christmas JOY

Quilt is 27" x 39" finished.

by Luella Dusek and Janice Vaine
Quilted by Marilyn Lange

Fabric requirements

Light Background	⅔ yard
Assorted Scraps	28–4½" x 2½"
Dark Background & Inner Border	⅓ yard
Final Border	½ yard
Binding	¼ yard
Backing	1 yard
Appliqué	Fat quarters in colors desired
Embellishment	Ribbons, embroidery floss, beads as desired

Cutting

Light Background:
3–12" x 12" squares

3–2½" x width of fabric strips
subcut 28–2½" x 2½"
2–2½" x 8½"

Assorted Scrap Flying Geese:
28–4½" x 2½"

Dark Background & Inner Border:
2–2½" x width of fabric" strip
subcut 28–2½" x 2½"
3–2" x width of fabric strips
subcut 2–2" x 31½"
2–2" x 16½"

Final Border:
3–4½" x width of fabric strips
subcut 2–4½" x 39½"
2–4½" x 19½"

Binding:
3–2½" x width of fabric strips

Use ¼" seam allowances.

1 Appliquéd Squares:

(A) Using a light box, trace the "B" wreath on page 41 onto an 8½" x 11" sheet of paper. Make 3 photocopies. Center and trace each letter, "J" (page 57), "O" (page 67), and "Y" (page 87) onto one of the photocopied wreaths.

(B) Appliqué the letter first, then the wreath, and ten bottom leaves of the wreath. Repeat for all three blocks.

(C) Using the Fishbone Stitch (page 98) and three strands of 6-stranded cotton embroidery floss, embroider the remaining six top leaves on each wreath.

(D) Using the Stem Stitch on page 112 and one strand of 6-stranded cotton embroidery floss, embroider veins on each of the appliquéd leaves.

(E) Make three Petal Flowers (page 104) as follows:

Make 24 large petals from 12–2¼" circles and 24 small petals from 12–1½" circles.

Make three Petal Flowers with the large petals and 3 Petal Flowers with the small petals.

Stitch a small flower on top of a large flower. Place on wreath and secure.

Appliqué a 1" circle to the center of each flower. Cover with beads.

(F) Press and trim blocks (page 34) to 8½" x 8½"

There are two different Flying Geese blocks. The construction of the two Flying Geese blocks is the same, but the placement of the Light and Dark Background squares will vary.
Decide where you will be placing the assorted Flying Geese blocks before making them.

2 **Flying Geese:** Draw diagonal lines on the back of all the Light and Dark 2½" Background squares. To make one Flying Geese block, sew 1–2½" Background square on the diagonal line to 1–4½" x 2½" Flying Geese rectangle. Trim ¼" away from the sewn line. Press to the corner to form a triangle. Sew another 1–2½" Background square on the diagonal line to the same rectangle. Trim and press to form the triangle. Follow the diagrams to make the two mirror image Flying Geese blocks.

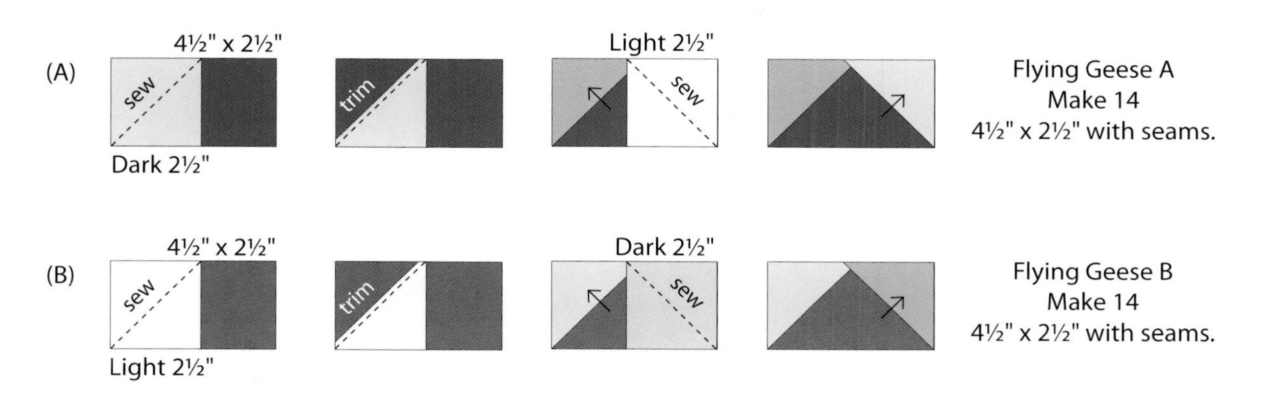

3 Follow the diagrams to assemble the quilt top. Sew the 3–2½" x width of fabric binding strips together. Layer, quilt and bind.

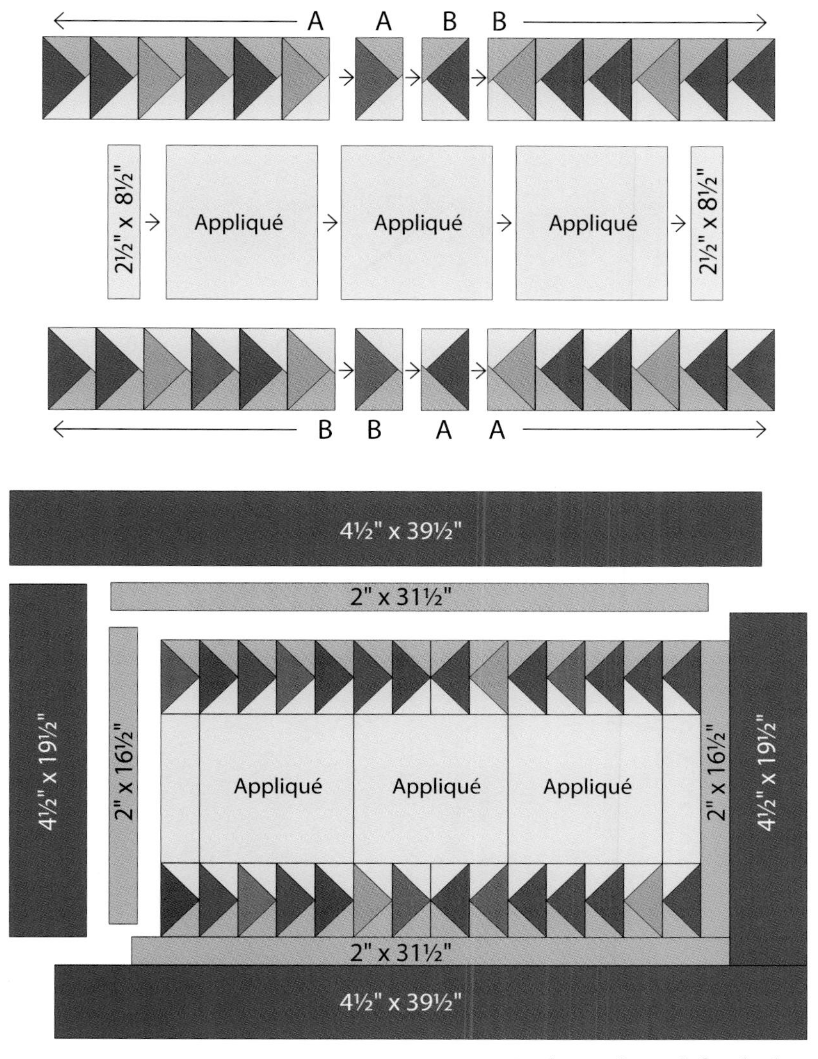

Quilt is 27" x 39" finished.

by Jo Ann Cridge and Janice Vaine

"A" is for Appliqué Small Pillow

Pillow is 9" x 9" finished.

Fabric requirements	Cutting
Embellished block background–Fat quarter*	10" x 10"
Setting Triangles–Fat quarter*	2–7" x 7" squares cut in half diagonally
Backing–Fat quarter*	9½" x 9½"
Binding–Fat quarter*	3–1⅛" x 21" strips, sew end to end
Pillow Form	8" x 8"
Lace	1 yard of 1" lace

Appliqué–Fat quarters in colors desired
Embellishment–Ribbons, embroidery floss, beads as desired

*Fat quarter–18" x 22"

Use ¼" seam allowances unless otherwise noted.

1 (A) Copy the A block on page 39, or the block of your choice, reducing to 50 percent. Appliqué and embellish the block. Trim on point to 5½" x 5½".

(B) Sew setting triangles to center block. Press away from the embellished block. Trim to 9½" x 9½" square.

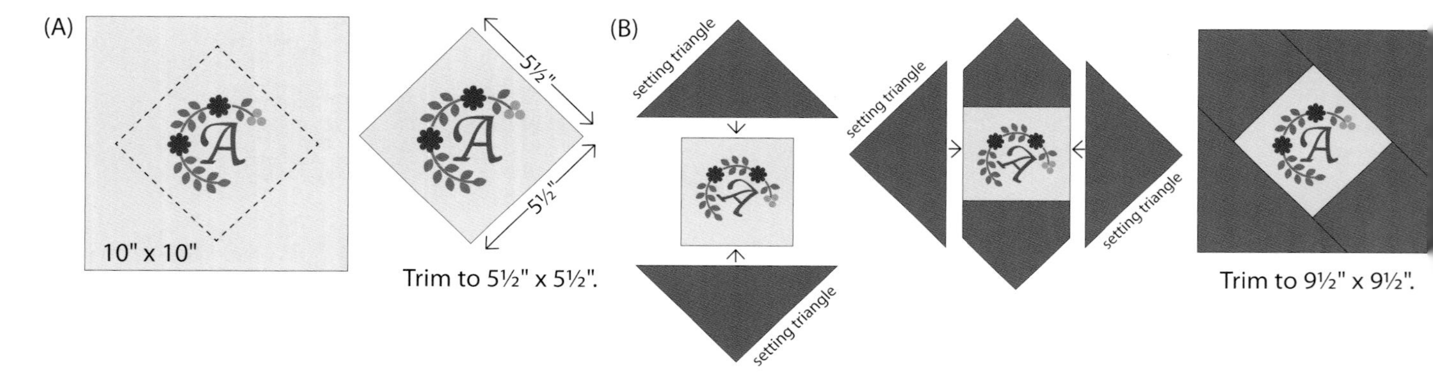

2 (A) Beginning in a corner, pin lace around the edge of the center block, mitering or gathering corners as desired. Sew lace to the block with a tiny zigzag stitch setting sewing machine to stitch width–1, stitch length–1.

(B) Place the pillow front and backing wrong sides together. Baste together leaving a 6" opening along bottom edge.

(C) Sew the single-fold binding around basted edges of the pillow front with a ⅜" seam allowance. Leave a 6" opening on the bottom edge. Insert pillow form. Sew opening closed. Finish attaching the binding.

(A)

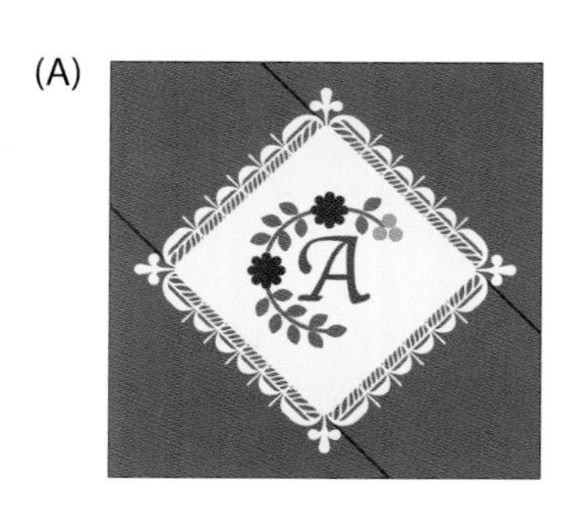

(B) pillow back

6" opening

(C)

6" opening

Pillow is 9" x 9" finished.

by Luella Dusek and Janice Vaine

Lavender Sachet

Sachet is 6" x 8" finished.

Fabric requirements	Cutting
Embellished block background– Fat quarter*	10" x 10"
Sachet Lower Back–Fat quarter*	5" x 6"
Center Strip–Fat quarter*	2–1" x 6"
Top of Sachet–Fat quarter*	2–10½" x 6"
Sachet Pillow–Fat quarter* of muslin	2–6" x 7"
Lace–½ yard of ⅝" lace	2–⅝" x 6"
Ribbon ties–	
1½ yards 7mm silk ribbon	3–12" lengths; 1–18" length
1 yard 4mm silk ribbon	3–12" lengths
Appliqué–Fat quarters in colors desired	
Embellishment–Ribbons, embroidery floss, beads as desired	

*Fat quarter–18" x 22"

Use ¼" seam allowances.

1 (A) Copy the B block on page 41, or the block of your choice, reducing to 50 percent. Appliqué and embellish the block. Trim block to 5" x 6".

(B) Fold Sachet top front in half right sides together. Stitch 2" down from folded top. Clip to seam. Turn right side out. Repeat with the Sachet back.

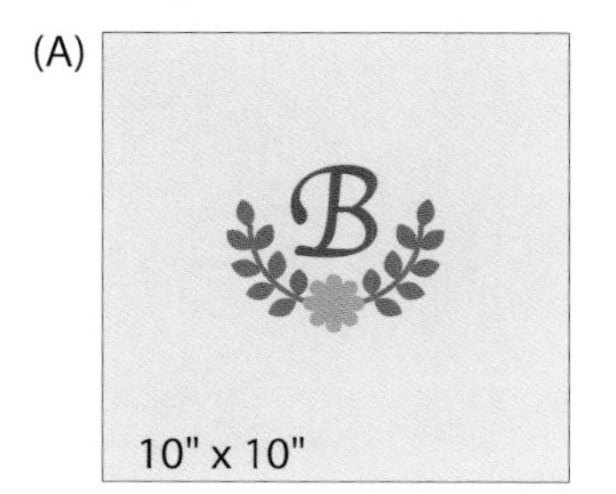

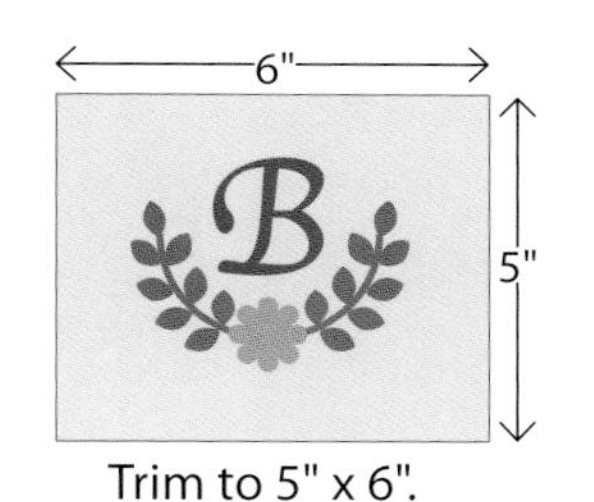

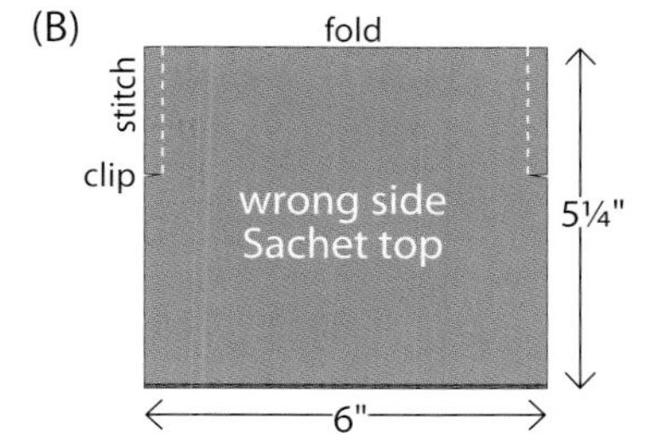

2 (A) Fold the 1" x 6" center strip in half, wrong sides together.

(B) Place folded strip between front and top, right sides together. Stitch with a ¼" seam. Press seam up.

(C) Add lace along top edge of strip using a tiny zigzag stitch, setting sewing machine to stitch width–1, stitch length–1. Repeat for back pieces.

(D) Place front and back right sides together. Stitch sides and bottom with a ¼" seam. Turn right side out. Make a sachet pillow with the muslin pieces, sewing around edges and leaving a small opening for stuffing. Stuff the sachet pillow with lavender. Sew opening closed. Insert into bag.

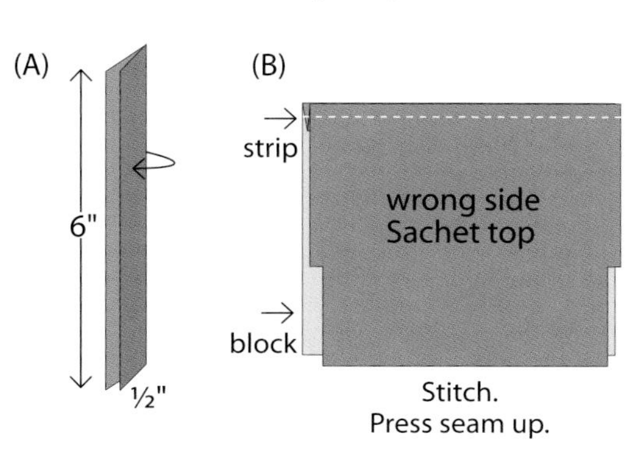

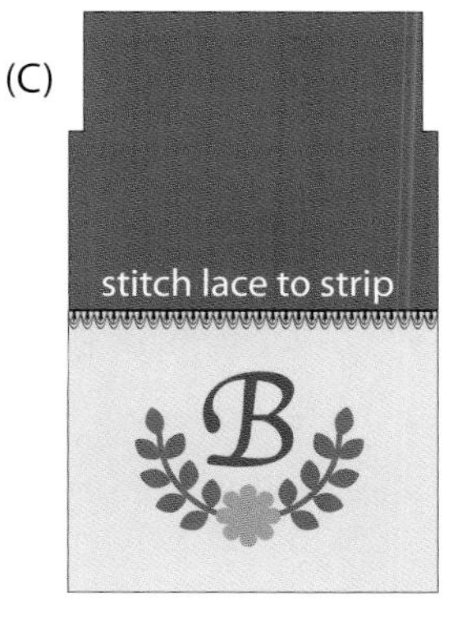

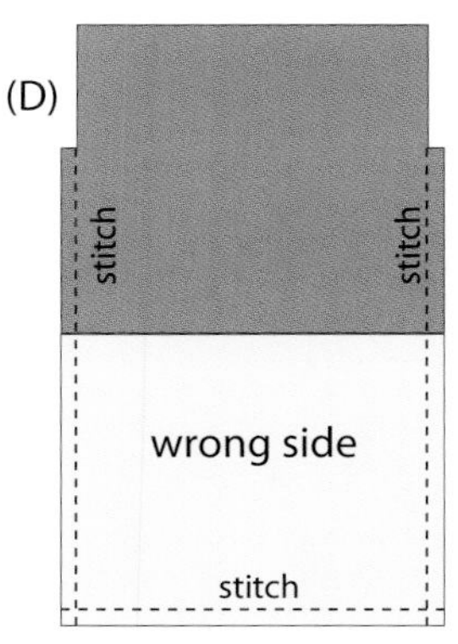

3 Lay the 3-12" lengths of 7mm and 3-12" lengths of 4mm ribbons together. Tie top of bag together with ribbons. Wrap the 18" length of 7mm ribbon around the tied 7mm and 4mm ribbons and tie a bow. Trim ends of ribbon on a diagonal to desired length.

by Luella Dusek and Janice Vaine

Needle & Pin Keeper

Needle and Pin Keeper is 4" round finished.

Fabric requirements	Cutting
Embellished block background–	
Fat quarter*	10" x 10"
Backing–Fat quarter*	6" circle
Center of Needle & Pin Keeper–	
⅛ yard felted wool or felt	¼" x 15"
Padding–Fat quarter* batting	4–5" circles
Template plastic–10" x 10"	2–4" circles
Foam core–6" x 6" of ¼"-thick	4" circle
Fabric glue	
Appliqué–Fat quarters in colors desired	
Embellishment–Ribbons, embroidery floss, beads as desired	

*Fat quarter–18" x 22"

Optional: pins to decorate outside edge of Needle & Pin Keeper

1

(A) Copy the C block on page 43, or the block of your choice, reducing to 50 percent. Appliqué and embellish the block. Center and trace a 6" circle around embellished block. Trim along traced line.

(B) Baste around outside edges of embellished front. Repeat on back piece.

(C) Center two pieces of batting on the wrong side of the front circle. Center template plastic circle on top of batting. Gather the basting stitches around the batting and template and secure stitching. *Repeat for back pieces.*

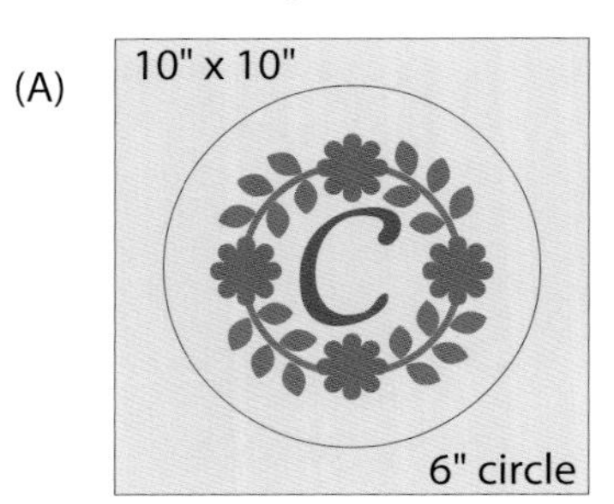

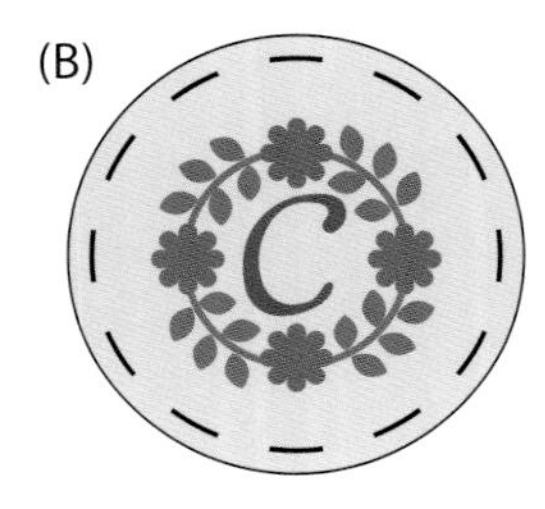

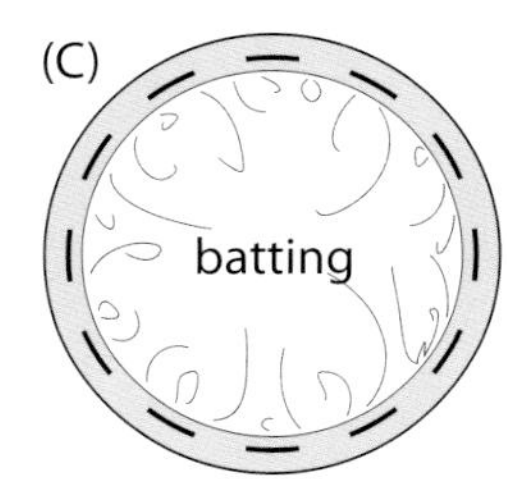

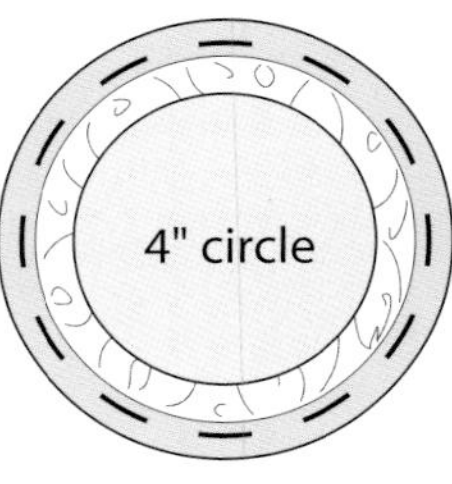

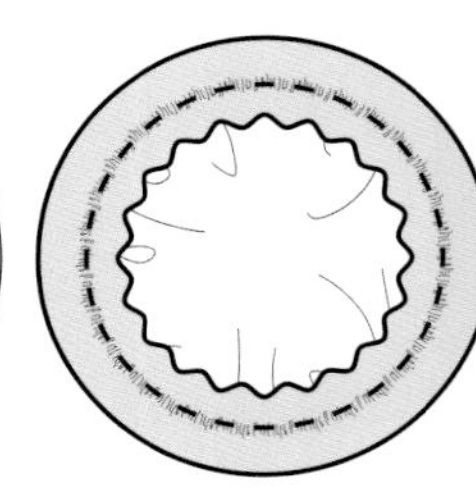

2

(A) Glue ¼" x 15" wool strip to side of foam core circle. Stitch seam together.

(B) Place the gathered side of the padded back circle on the bottom of the foam core. Appliqué to the wool.

(C) Place the gathered side of the embellished padded top circle on top of the foam core. Appliqué to the top of the wool.

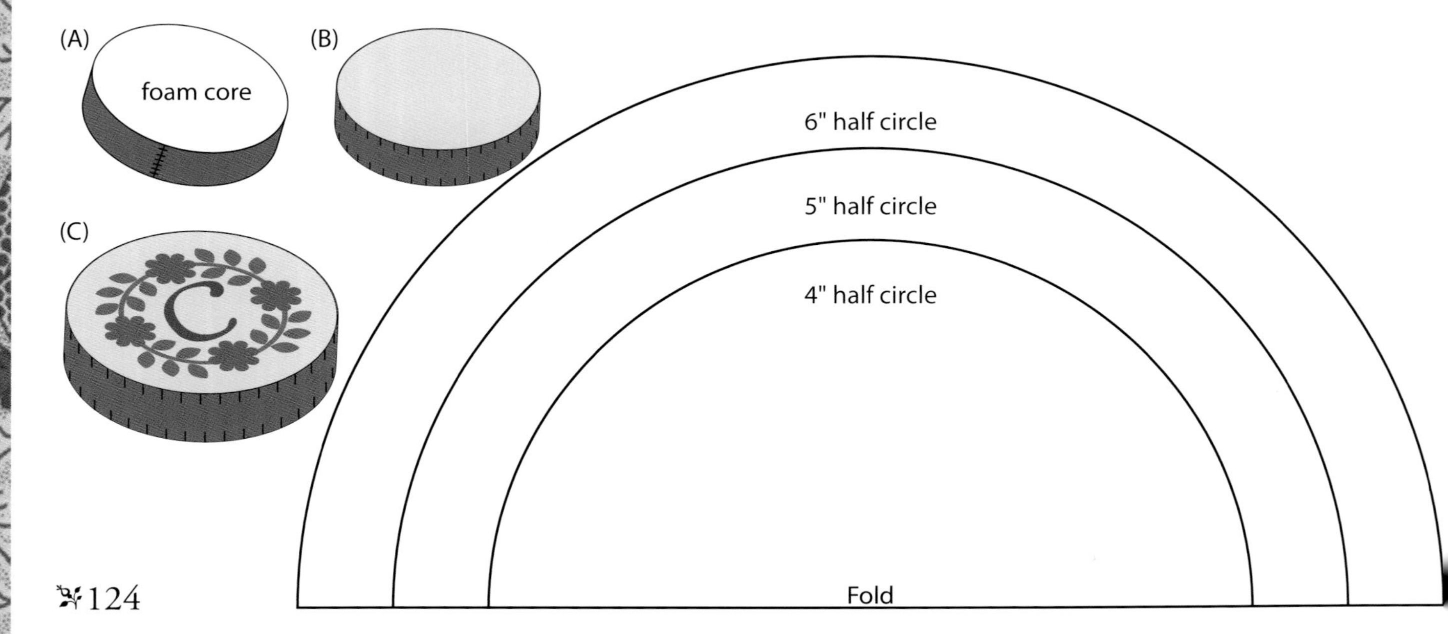

by Luella Dusek and Janice Vaine
Quilted by Marilyn Lange

One Block Quilt

Quilt is 18" x 18" finished.

Fabric requirements	Cutting
Embellished block background– Fat quarter*	12" x 12"
1st Inner Border–Fat quarter*	2–1" x 10½"; 2–1" x 9½"
2nd Inner Border–Fat quarter*	2–1½" x 12½"; 2–1½" x 10½"
Final Border–Fat quarter*	2–3½" x 12½"; 2–3½" x 18½"
Binding–Fat quarter*	4–1⅛" x 21"; sew end to end
Backing–Fat quarter*	
Appliqué–Fat quarters in colors desired	
Embellishment–Ribbons, embroidery floss, beads as desired	

*Fat quarter–18" x 22"

Use ¼" seam allowances.

1. (A) Appliqué and embellish the center block as desired. Trim to 9½" x 9½".
   (B) Add 1st Inner Border. *Always add side borders first then the top and bottom borders. Always press away from the block center.*
   (C) Add 2nd Inner Border.
   (D) Add the Final Border. Layer, quilt, and bind.

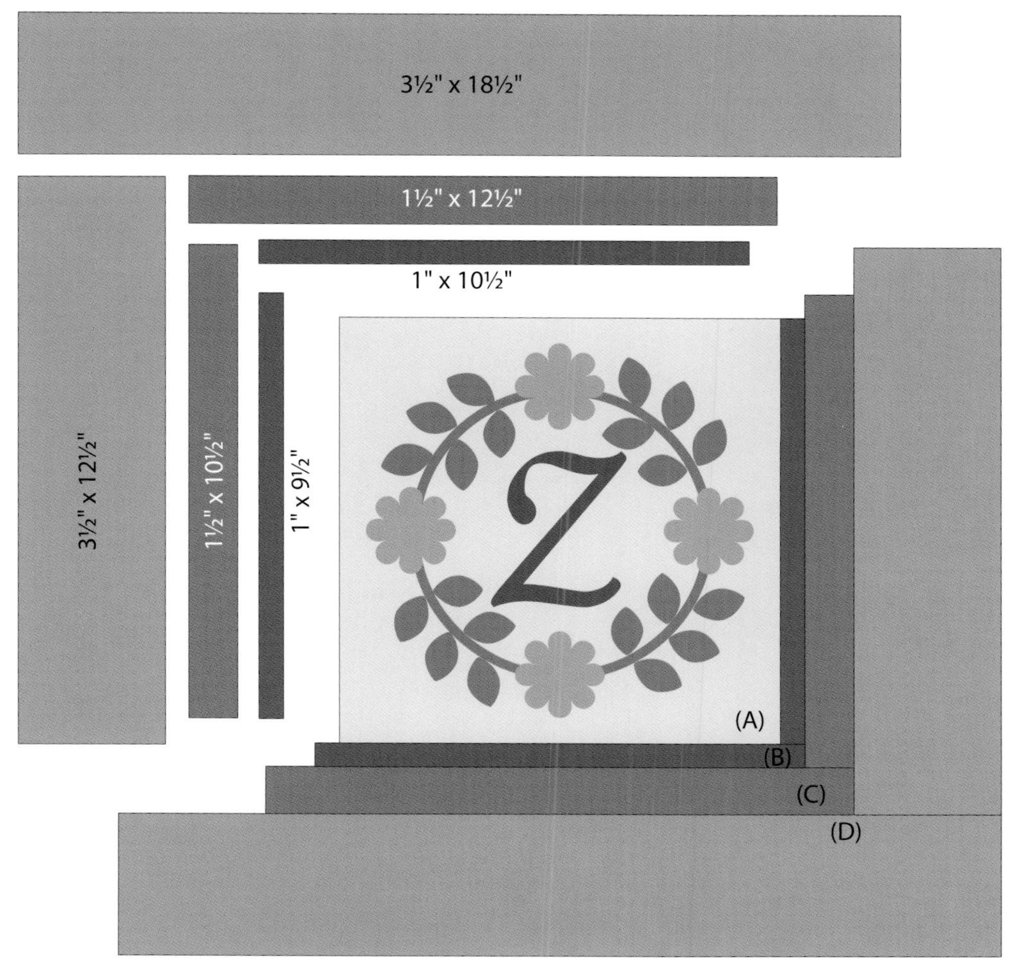

Quilt is 18" x 18" finished.

Enlargement & Reduction Chart

Photocopier Settings

Current block size down left hand column. New block size across the top.
Find where column and row meet for amount to reduce or enlarge original block.

	1"	2"	3"	4"	5"	6"	7"	8"	9"	10"	11"	12"
1"	100%	200%	300%	400%	500%	600%	700%	800%	900%	1000%	1100%	1200%
2"	50%	100%	150%	200%	250%	300%	350%	400%	450%	500%	550%	600%
3"	33%	66%	100%	133%	166%	200%	233%	266%	300%	333%	366%	400%
4"	25%	50%	75%	100%	125%	150%	175%	200%	225%	250%	275%	300%
5"	20%	40%	60%	80%	100%	120%	140%	160%	180%	200%	220%	240%
6"	17%	33%	50%	67%	83%	100%	117%	133%	150%	167%	183%	200%
7"	14%	29%	43%	57%	71%	86%	100%	114%	129%	143%	157%	171%
8"	13%	25%	38%	50%	63%	75%	88%	100%	113%	125%	138%	150%
9"	11%	22%	33%	44%	56%	67%	78%	89%	100%	111%	122%	133%
10"	10%	20%	30%	40%	50%	60%	70%	80%	90%	100%	110%	120%
11"	9%	18%	27%	36%	45%	55%	64%	73%	82%	91%	100%	109%
12"	8%	17%	25%	33%	42%	50%	58%	67%	75%	83%	92%	100%

Use the following formula if the size you want is not on the table above:
Block size wanted (divided by) **Current Block size** = **Percent to Enlarge or Reduce**

Example: To enlarge: Size you want = 12" and Current size = 4"
12 divided by 4 = 3 (answer times 100 = 300%)
To reduce: Size you want = 7" and Current size = 12"
7 divided by 12 = .58 (answer times 100 = 58%)

Resources

Landauer Publishing, LLC
3100 101st Street, Urbandale, IA 50322 USA
1-800-557-2144, www.landauercorp.com

Marilyn Lange Quilts
6191 Cherrywood Drive, Ypsilanti, MI 48197 USA
734-483-5690, mlangequilts@yahoo.com

Mill Hill
N162 Highway 35, Stoddard, WI 54658 USA
1-800-356-9516, www.millhill.com

Morgan Hoops
8040 Erie Avenue, Chanhassen, MN 55217 USA
612-387-2183, www.nosliphoops.com

Quilter's Fancy
P.O. Box 457, Cortland, OH 44410 USA
1-866-953-0722, www.quiltersfancy.com

Superior Threads
87 East 2580 South, St. George, UT 84790 USA
1-800-499-1777, www.superiorthreads.com

The Gentle Art
P.O. Box 670, New Albany, OH 43054 USA
www.thegentleart.com

Thimbles by TJ Lane
P.O. Box 83108, Lincoln, NE 68501 USA
1-866-647-9673, www.thimbles2fit.com

United Notions/Moda Fabrics
13800 Hutton Drive, Dallas, TX 75234 USA
1-800-527-9447, www.unitednotions.com

YLI Corporation
1439 Dave Lyle Blvd., Rock Hill, SC 29730 USA
1-803-628-5979, www.ylicorp.com

Acknowledgements

For all those who made this book a possibility and reality, my sincere and heartfelt thanks. To the Landauer Publishing team: Jeramy Landauer, Kitty Jacobson, Jeri Simon, Sue Voegtlin, Laurel Albright, McB McManus, Julie Ryan, and Eric Stifel; to designer and technical illustrator, Lisa Christensen; to the needle artists whose loving stitches grace these pages, my Mom (Luella Dusek), Jo Ann Cridge, Sonnie Cridge, Gena Holland, and Lynn Rogers; to Lissa Alexander and Moda Fabrics for providing fabrics for the projects and book pages; to longarm quilter, Marilyn Lange for adding the finishing touch to the quilts; and to all the suppliers who supported this project, including Morgan Hoops, Quilter's Fancy, Superior Threads, The Gentle Art, and YLI Corporation.

And my forever love to my best friend, partner, and love of my life, Joe, for all your encouragement, support, patience and the love only a husband could give (particularly while working on a book).

Thank you all for sharing in this journey. *Janice Vaine*

About the Author

Janice Vaine

Born in Pittsburgh, Pennsylvania, Jan has resided in Jacksonville, Florida for the past 36 years. Married to her husband of 30 years, they currently share their home and lifes with Doogan, an effervescent 3-year-old Wheaton terrier, Sophia, an 8-year-old mixed breed sophisticated lady, and three curious kitties, Tigger, Josie, and Cookie. There is never a dull moment in their household!

Jan has a love of vintage embroidery and antique quilts. She studies them for their methods and techniques and to learn how the early stitchers created their designs using embroidery, stumpwork and ribbonwork. These features, as well as the lovely handwork, are what inspire Jan to create her fresh new designs. Taking on the challenge of miniature work and downsizing vintage pieced and appliqué quilts have also added to her design inspiration. The old is new again.

In 2003, Jan was invited by Elly Sienkiewicz to be the guest designer for the ancillary projects in Elly's book, "Baltimore Elegance". In 2004, her love of sewing and designing blossomed into her pattern company, The Graham Cracker Collection (www.grahamcrackercollection.com). And in 2011, Jan's first book, "The Art of Elegant Hand Embroidery, Embellishment and Appliqué" was published.

Jan enjoys teaching and sharing her love of needlearts with her students. She brings 46 years of sewing and needlework experience to her work and classes. She is an experienced seamstress, quilter, appliqué enthusiast, pattern designer, and teacher. Her teaching credentials over the past 20 years include the The Elly Sienkiewicz Appliqué Academy in Willliamsburg, Virginia; the Spring and Fall International Quilt Markets, the International Quilt Festival in Houston, Texas; quilt guild retreats; and her local quilt and sewing shops.

An Old Irish Blessing

May there always be work for your hands to do.
May your purse always hold a coin or two.
May the sun always shine on your windowpane.
May a rainbow be certain to follow each rain.
May the hand of a friend always be near you.
May God fill your heart with gladness to cheer you.